CONTENTS

HINDU RITUAL AN

Dermot Killingley
Werner Menski
Shirley Firth

S. Y. Killingley
Newcastle upon Tyne

The Sanskrit Tradition in the Modern World (STIMW) 2
Series Editor: Dermot Killingley

In this series:

Yvonne Williams and Michael McElvaney, *Aurobindo and Zaehner on the Bhagavad-Gītā*

Published by S. Y. Killingley. Distributed by Grevatt & Grevatt,
9 Rectory Drive, Newcastle upon Tyne NE3 1XT

Set by Grevatt & Grevatt and printed in Great Britain by Jasprint Ltd.,
12 Tower Road, Glover District 11, Washington, Tyne & Wear NE37 2SH

British Library Cataloguing in Publication Data

Killingley, Dermot, *1935-*
Hindu ritual and society. - (The Sanskrit tradition in the modern world; 2)
I. Title II. Menski, Werner III. Firth, Shirley
IV. Series
294.5

ISBN 0 947722 06 8

Price: £8.95 plus carriage charge:
UK: 15% (single-copy orders) or 10% (multiple-copy orders)
Overseas: 30%. Extra £8 bank charges with non-sterling payments
20% trade discount plus above p & p to UK booksellers only

This book has been non-commercially published and priced. It may be bought direct from Grevatt & Grevatt or through general distributors.

The publisher gratefully acknowledges the kind co-operation of the following in advertising this publication:
The British Association for the History of Religions
The Group for Ethnic Minority Studies, School of Oriental and African Studies.

INTRODUCTION

Dermot Killingley

> That's all the facts when you come to brass tacks:
> Birth, and copulation, and death.
>
> (T. S. Eliot, *Sweeney Agonistes*)

> tvaṃ ca māṃ śruti-saṃskāraiḥ sarvaiḥ saṃskartum arhasi,
> saṃskāra-rahitaṃ janma yataś ca paśuvat smṛtam.
> 'Please prepare me with all the Vedic saṃskāras, because birth without saṃskāras is said to be brutish.'
>
> (The newly-born Skanda to Viśvāmitra, *SkP* 1, 2, 29, 146b-147a)

> saṃskāro nāma sa bhavati yasmiñ jāte padārtho bhavati yogyaḥ kasya cid arthasya.
> 'A saṃskāra is that on whose occurrence a thing becomes fit for some purpose.'
>
> (Śabarasvāmin on *Jaiminīya-Sūtra* 3, 1, 3)

Life, as a series of biological events, is shared by humankind with other animals. By means of rituals, we integrate these events into an order, whether this order is regarded as sacred or as an aspect of the profane world. A ritual of this kind, known to anthropology as a rite of passage (Van Gennep 1960), is called in the brahmanical tradition a *saṃskāra*, sometimes rather narrowly translated 'sacrament' or 'purification', or more evocatively 'polishing' (Gold 1989: 81); we can translate it comprehensively as 'process', since the word can refer, outside the ritual context, to processes such as polishing or cooking. A saṃskāra makes a person fit for the stage of life (including life beyond death) which he or she is entering; and a life marked throughout by the proper saṃskāras is called *saṃskṛta:* processed, cultivated, fit for men and gods, like the Sanskrit language itself. What saṃskāras one undergoes, and in what form, depends on one's caste; saṃskāras are thus markers of social categories.

The three papers in this book were presented at the annual seminars on The Sanskrit Tradition in the Modern World at the University of Newcastle upon Tyne. In revising them for publication, all three authors have benefited greatly from the discussions which took place at the seminars. We are especially grateful to Dr. John Brockington and Dr. Siew-Yue Killingley.

My own paper deals with caste, the system of social divisions whose membership depends on birth, and which are marked, among other ways, by differences in ritual. These divisions are South Asian rather than peculiarly Hindu; but they receive ideological sanction from the brahmanical tradition (cf. Dumont 1972: 247-58). Caste has been identified as 'the fundamental institution of Hinduism' (Weber 1958: 29) and even as 'the South Asian social system' (Klass 1980), so that it seems to eclipse other topics which are also relevant to South Asian society, such as village, lineage and family. My paper explores the complex relation between caste and the tradition, and the ways in which this relation has been modified in modern times. In the other two papers, Werner Menski and Shirley Firth deal with the two series of saṃskāras which are the most publicly visible and the most concerned with the social order: those surrounding marriage and death. While both these papers use material from ancient and modern India, they are focused on the ways in which rituals are put into practice and modified by Hindus in Britain. Each of them testifies to the strength of tradition and the desire of British Hindus to ensure that the rituals are properly carried out and understood; each of them also has a practical concern. Menski describes how English law finds itself obliged to ascribe some legal status to Hindu marriage rituals, and consequently to know what constitutes a valid Hindu marriage. Firth, in describing the needs of Hindu families and the pandits who advise them, indicates how the British health care professions can help Hindus to deal with death and bereavement.

It is not for nothing that marriage and death rituals, the extremes of auspiciousness and inauspiciousness, are chosen here from among the range of saṃskāras attending the Hindu life-cycle. Sixteen or even forty are sometimes listed (Kane 1941: 193f; Pandey 1969: 19-23), and those surrounding pregnancy and birth have already been studied with special reference to Hindus in Britain (McDonald in Burghart 1987: 50-66). But while other saṃskāras take place in the home, and give little occasion for public spectacle, marriage and death require a public procession, from the bridegroom's home to the bride's (or to a hired hall), and from the dead person's home to the cremation ground (or crematorium). It is on these two occasions that the marriage circle—the endogamous group which is basic to caste—comes together (Klass 1980: 97). Marriage is 'at the heart of Hindu society' (Tambiah 1973: 223), and all Hindu ritual can be seen as a preparation for death (Stevenson 1920: 136; below, p. 55). Both link the world of the living to that of the ancestors, since marriage makes possible the birth of legitimate sons, who can perform the death rituals and ancestral offerings.

Any ritual, even if its precise pattern is unique, is made up of elements which have been used before, much as any piece of speech we utter is made up of words and structures learnt from previous utterances, though the utterance itself may be unique. In this way ritual, like language, links its participants with other participants in similar activities, thus showing that they are members of a society.

There are many ways of performing what is recognizably the same ritual, as we may observe in any society when attending weddings or funerals, or less climactic rituals such as graduations or birthday parties. Differences may depend on region, on the wealth, class or age of the participants, and so on. Opinions on the proper procedure may differ among the principal persons involved, their relatives, and various functionaries such as priests, undertakers, or photographers; such differences may be resolved, and a procedure arrived at, either by prior negotiation or by covert or open tussles on the spot. In Hindu society, and indeed in South Asian society as a whole, one of the factors differentiating ritual procedures is the status inherited by the principal or principals from their parents.

The Sanskrit śāstras have long sought to codify such differences. For instance, we are told that a burial mound is to be as high as the upstretched arms for a kṣatriya, the mouth for a brahmin, the hips for a woman, the thighs for a vaiśya, and the knees for a śūdra (*ŚBr* 13, 8, 3, 11). This passage illustrates several of the themes of the present book. First, it envisages the burial of the calcined bones rather than their disposal in a river as at present, reminding us that the ritual tradition is not immutable. It lays down different rules for different classes of people, in terms of the four varṇas, though for many centuries these have not been, if they ever were, the actual divisions of society (cf. p. 16). In its choice of parts of the body as measurements for burial mounds, it alludes to the hymn of the Man (*ṚV* 10, 90; cf. p. 11), the locus classicus for varṇa. At the same time it exalts the kṣatriya above the brahmin, contrary to the usual ranking order of the varṇas. Finally, the four varṇas seem to consist only of men; women are treated as a separate group, and assigned to a part of the body appropriate to their erotic and procreative function. Let us examine in turn the topics which the passage raises.

The first topic, change, is not an accident which attacks ritual from the outside, but is intrinsic to it as it is to language; and if change occurs, so also does variety, since not all members of a society will change their practices simultaneously. The śāstras recognize the possibility of change, but tend to formalize it by reference to the cosmic cycle of ages; practices prescribed in the Veda but no longer approved being regarded as lawful in a perfect world but forbidden in the Kali Yuga, the degenerate present age. They are also familiar with differences between regions and families; such differences are built into the very structure of the literature, with its different Vedic schools, its sūtras named after different ṛṣis, and its commentaries, digests and ritual manuals prevailing in different regions.

Nor is change peculiar to the modern period; but modern conditions, especially in travel and communications, have accelerated it and also made us more aware of it. My own paper shows how changing attitudes have led to re-evaluations of caste which attempt to reassert rather than to reject tradition. The other two papers show that change often involves an attempt to standardize practice with reference to the śāstras, though these may reveal diversity rather than uniformity. Even such adjustments to British conditions as the inclusion of the registry wedding as part of the complex of Hindu marriage rituals (p. 47), or the ending of mourning observances with the cremation (p. 79), do not imply that those who make them are unaware of the traditional rules. Change in Britain is continuous with, and facilitated by, the change and variety in the South Asian past, both ancient and modern; it need not mean getting more like the British and less like Indians (p. 34). Some innovations, such as the foundation of temples and the growing use of home and commercial videos from India, reinforce attachment to tradition while also modifying it. Moreover, changes in Britain can be matched with those observed in urban India (p. 52).

In Britain we find a new kind of ritual specialist, referred to as *priest* or *pandit*, who combines the traditional roles of the pūjārī, responsible for the worship of the images in the local temple, and the purohit who conducts saṃskāras for the families who form his clientèle. He may have to adapt his practice to different ethnic groups (p. 49), and also perform death rituals, traditionally the function not of the purohit but of the despised mahābrāhmaṇa; his wish to provide for the needs of local Hindus must be reconciled with his sense of the inauspiciousness of death rituals (pp. 81f). The priest or pandit is also taking on a pastoral role, providing advice on ritual and moral matters for Hindus living in an undefined area surrounding the temple, who are as it were his parishioners; they may also expect him to follow Hindu norms of dress and diet more strictly and more often than they, serving as their proxy in orthopraxy.

In these circumstances, the priest is both agent and regulator of change, negotiating with his clients, particularly the older women of the family. Variant rituals in different British cities depend on material and personal resources, on the ethnicity of the participants, and on the views and persuasive power of individual priests. To cite one example: whereas in Southampton, which has had a temple since 1984, the funeral journey goes straight from the home to the crematorium (pp. 73, 77), the custom in Newcastle is to make a détour to bring the coffin to the temple door—significantly no further. This is part of a general tendency among overseas Hindus to make the temple the focus of religious life and the location of rituals.

The next topic raised by the *ŚBr* passage, the differentiation of the varṇas, is occasionally important in present-day ritual, even in Britain. First, there is a marked preference, if not a requirement, for a brahmin rather than any other officiant wherever possible. Second, there is some differentiation in death rituals (pp. 64, 79). But the distinction between the twice-born and śūdras, so crucial in the śāstras, is scarcely apparent; and the sacred thread, instead of being a prerequisite for participation in certain rituals, is something that can be manufactured ad hoc (p. 75). It is more in the realm of ideology than of practice that varṇa is important in the modern world.

The position of brahmins, which our passage showed was not absolutely superior to that of kṣatriyas, remains ambivalent. If Comte's and Bankim's picture of the altruistic lawgiver is absurdly idealized (pp. 22, 25), the more prevalent, and indeed more historical picture of the brahmin using his position as lawgiver and controller of tradition to gain wealth and power under every régime leaves certain points out of account. It is on the ritual dimension that brahmins as such rank high; for other purposes they may be subordinate to non-brahmins, as K. M. Banerjea saw (p. 21). Even their ritual functions do not always imply superiority; brahmins in Vedic times, according to Menski, were involved in marriage rituals as 'ritual scapegoats' (p. 35); and in death rituals this function is still apparent (pp. 52, 57, 81f). However, we must not forget the over-representation of brahmins in the professions. This is reflected in the Indian judiciary's bias towards brahmanical norms (p. 43), which is distinct from the kind of élite bias that one might find in any judiciary.

We come finally to the special position of women. While they are recognized as guardians of the non-śāstric, laukika traditions, they are excluded by the śāstras from playing a leading role in saṃskāras, and even from undergoing saṃskāras in which Vedic mantras are used (*Manu* 2, 66); thus even women who belong by birth to the twice-born varṇas are treated for ritual purposes as śūdras. A woman is never independent, we are told; for her, marriage takes the place of initiation with the sacred thread (*Manu* 5, 148; 2, 67; here, the text must be thinking of women of the twice-born varṇas only). We do, however, find women playing leading roles in Britain, at least as a makeshift (p. 54). It is well known that the funeral pyre can only be lit by a son or other close male relative, and that women do not follow the body to the cremation ground (just as they do not in parts of traditional British society). Yet as soon as we utter such a generalization with reference to Hinduism, we know there must be exceptions. There is, for instance, a class of women in the Panjab hills who do not marry, and who take on some of the roles of men, including the possibility of attending cremations (Phillimore 1991). When Rajiv Gandhi's widow and daughter prepared his pyre, perhaps they were just doing what seemed right in the circumstances, drawing selectively on a ritual tradition which is so vast that it can only be used selectively. It was certainly not unprecedented; Sharma (1971: 171) gives a poignant description by a Panjabi Khatri woman of how she herself lit the pyre of her husband's niece in Delhi, as directed by the funeral priest, because no one else would do it.

What does a saṃskāra do? Is it primarily a social, a legal or a religious act? Ancient Indian ritual theory says it effects something adṛṣṭa, 'unseen', which will affect a person's destiny in this world or elsewhere; this view is still held (pp. 48, 62, 81f). In India, Hindu marriage rituals effect a legal status; they can also have this effect in English law (p. 32). For the parties themselves, the rituals may be essential for their sense of being married (pp. 44, 46f), and some pandits have apparently held that the spouses' knowledge that they are married is the essence of marriage (Derrett 1976: 179).

The law takes an interest in marriage rituals because it is often only through rituals of some kind that people can be married. On the other hand it has little concern with death rituals, once it has been established that death has occurred and that hygiene will not be endangered. If uncertainty arises as to whether someone is dead or not, the witnesses to be called are experts in medicine, not in ritual. Whereas, then, matrimony is a status which is effected by a wedding, death occurs independently of ritual, and death rituals effect something else: the welfare of the deceased in another world, perhaps, or comfort for the survivors. Death belongs to nature, marriage (whether in the sense of wedding or of matrimony) to culture.

Yet this opposition needs examination. It has been argued that

> Bodily experiences are themselves culturally defined and derive their meaning as *human* experiences from the cultural definition given to them. In

> this sense one may say that, at least for some purposes, nature is itself a construct of culture (Das 1985: 196).

We can never, as Eliot's vulgar character Sweeney supposed, 'come to brass tacks'; and we should not assume that while marriage is essentially a cultural construct to which the natural fact of copulation has been subordinated, death is a mere natural event which exists apart from culture, except at a biological level at which human experience is ignored. The brahmanical tradition, while recognizing that the death saṃskāras are occasioned by the natural event of death, in some ways treats death as being effected by the saṃskāras. Thus, although physical functions have already ceased, the departure of the prāṇas is effected ritually, by the breaking of the skull or the symbolic breaking of a pot (see esp. p. 70). This explains why some informants say that cremation during the critical period of pañcaka, rather than death during that period, is dangerous (p. 71). The use of the term *sahamaraṇa*, literally 'death with [the husband]', to refer to the act of a wife who burns herself on her husband's funeral pyre, implies that the husband's death is not accomplished until he is cremated. Accordingly, the wife is not a widow, and would only become one if she did not perform sahamaraṇa; she goes to the pyre dressed as a bride (Leslie 1991).

Since cremation traditionally follows within twenty-four hours of physical death, and often sooner, it is not unreasonable to treat death as a single series of processes which starts with the cessation of physical functions and continues with the cremation and even subsequent stages. Modern conditions, including not only bureaucratic procedures but also the desire of relatives to come from distant places (which affects middle-class families in India as well as overseas), put a temporal gap between death and the funeral, threatening the traditional hegemony of the ritual over the natural. The uncomprehending attitude of some hospital staff to pre-death rituals (p. 61-3) may have the same effect.

Negotiations over ritual procedure, therefore, result not only from different traditions of practice but from different views of the purpose of ritual. The timing that a family selects for a wedding for social reasons may be wrong from the pandit's point of view, or require remedial rituals (p. 48). Pandits may recite texts that are inappropriate from the point of view of the unseen, but provide comfort for mourners (pp. 75, 77). Such negotiation is still going on. Relations between castes are also subject to negotiation, and this includes radical reinterpretations of the texts which give them śāstric sanction (pp. 25-31).

VARṆA AND CASTE IN HINDU APOLOGETIC

Dermot Killingley

Introduction

So much primary and secondary material is already available about nineteenth-century and twentieth-century views on caste that another paper may seem superfluous. The reason for attempting it is that many sources on the subject, both primary and secondary, ignore the complexities of caste, and treat it as if the various topics of endogamy, ritual purity, untouchability, brahminhood, varṇa and so on were one phenomenon, known as caste, and familiar under that name to both writer and reader without further explanation. Sometimes the apparent convenience of the name *caste* has detracted from clarity of expression and even of thought, so that it is uncertain to the reader, and perhaps also to the writer, which of these topics is being referred to. In this way, for instance, a passage in which Keshub Chunder Sen speaks of the innate purity of humanity can be quoted as 'a terrible indictment on the so-called doctrine of untouchability' (Sen 1950: 271), though it says nothing about untouchables. The word *caste* has also been applied outside South Asia as the name of a supposed type of social organization, inadequately defined, its use being further complicated by the history of its Spanish cognate *casta* in Latin America (Pitt-Rivers 1971). This paper seeks to clarify Indian and other discourse on caste by concentrating on one distinction which is frequently obscured in English, and sometimes in Indian languages.

The distinction between varṇa and jāti

Varṇa is a key concept in the complex of ideas known as dharma. The term *varṇāśrama-dharma,* which is often closely associated with the notion of Hindu orthodoxy and invoked by those claiming to be orthodox, sums up a view of society in which each person, or at least each man, has a place in a two-dimensional grid whose axes are the four āśramas, or stages of life, and the four varṇas. Another concept, caste, is a key for the understanding of several aspects of Hindu life, including marriage patterns, kinship, food rules, ritual, and party politics.

The distinction between varṇa and caste is well known to anthropologists and others specializing in South Asian society, even if it is ignored by some authors whose approach to the study of India is primarily through Sanskrit literature. A modern Indian anthropologist has said:

> The varṇa-model has produced a wrong and distorted image of caste (Srinivas 1962: 66).

Vincent Smith, in a work first published in 1919, wrote in the same vein:

> Nobody can understand the caste system until he has freed himself from the mistaken notion based on the current interpretation of the so-called Institutes of Manu, that there were 'four original castes' (Smith 1958: 62).

'And yet it is a common and ingrained practice, resulting from a misconception about these two utterly different things and their properties, to superimpose on each of them the character and attributes of the other, failing to distinguish the two and coupling truth with untruth.'[1] Sanskritists, even though they may have been aware of the distinction, have not always made it clear. Bühler (1886) regularly translates both *varṇa* and *jāti* as 'caste', though he adds the original word in brackets. Monier-Williams' dictionary entry for *varṇa*, after 'colour' and related meanings, gives

> class of men, tribe, order, caste...more properly applicable to the four principal classes described in Manu's code...the more modern word for 'caste' being *jāti* (Monier-Williams 1899: 924).

Even if we remember that 'modern' to a nineteenth-century indologist can describe anything later than the Veda, this is not very helpful, though if we know the distinction already we can see that Monier-Williams has it in mind. Winternitz (1927: 66) refers to and enumerates 'the four castes', and in the next sentence implies the possibility of at least five 'lower castes'; in the former phrase, *caste* must mean 'varṇa', while in the latter it cannot. Many other writers regularly use the word *caste* when what they mean is clearly varṇa (e.g. Edgerton 1944; Hacker 1958), which is symptomatic of the traditional detachment of indology from the facts of South Asian society.

The usual Sanskrit word for what I have hitherto referred to as 'caste' is *jāti*, and related words are used in the same sense in many modern South Asian languages. To avoid the possibility of confusion in the ensuing discussion, I shall avoid the ambiguous (and also foreign) word *caste*, and use *jāti* instead. This does not mean that *caste* should necessarily be avoided elsewhere, as Mandelbaum (1970) does. On the contrary, I hope to clarify the well-established use of this word in the sense of *jāti*. I shall review the distinction between the concepts of varṇa and jāti, before going on to discuss the relation between them, the ways they have been used in nineteenth-century and twentieth-century discourse on Hinduism, and some of the ways in which confusion between them has been exploited in a creative

1 tathāpy anyonyasminn anyonyātmakatām anyonya-dharmāṃś cādhyasyetaretarāvivekenātyanta-viviktayor dharma-dharminor mithyā-jñāna-nimittaḥ satyānṛte mithunīkrtya...naisargiko 'yaṃ loka-vyavahāraḥ (Śaṅkara, introduction to *VS*). Śaṅkara is talking about the self and the not-self, but his words are applicable to more mundane forms of wrong knowledge.

reinterpretation of Hindu dharma.

Jāti refers to an indefinite number of divisions in South Asian society, characterized by heredity, endogamy, commensality, an actual or attributed common occupation, and actual or attributed peculiarities of diet. Jātis are ranked in a hierarchy, in which superiority of one jāti to others is marked by avoidance of contact of various kinds, notably acceptance of food and water.

The patterns of avoidance are so complex, however, that it is not always possible to arrive at an undisputed ranking order. For instance, if the first of two jātis does not accept food from the second, this places the first above the second. However, there may be a third jāti which accepts food from the second but not the first, thus placing the second above the first (e.g. Mayer 1960: 39). Moreover, a jāti can rise in the hierarchy if the jātis above it start to accept food from it; this usually requires a change in its dietary and ritual rules, and at the same time it may cease to accept food or water where it formerly did. It is also possible for a jāti to fall in the hierarchy, when other jātis cease to accept food or water from it.

If part of a jāti discontinues intermarriage with the rest of the jāti and becomes a separate endogamous group, and if it also ceases to eat with or accept food from the rest of the jāti, it thereby becomes a separate jāti; such a change may be accompanied by changes in diet, ritual and occupation (e.g. Mandelbaum 1970: II, 493-6). If, on the other hand, the boundaries of endogamy and commensality which formerly separated two jātis are consistently ignored, the two have thereby merged. The number of jātis is therefore not static; and since there will always be borderline cases where fission or merger may or may not be considered to have been accomplished, it is in principle impossible to count the number of jātis that exist. There are certainly several hundred; three thousand is a reasonable figure which is sometimes given, but cannot claim to be exact. Each jāti belongs to a particular region of South Asia, though it may of course spread to other regions through migration. Thus the inventory of jātis, so far as it can be compiled at all, varies geographically, so that in a given district the number of jātis may only be a matter of dozens.

Moreover, a group which is treated by others as one jāti may be treated by its own members as several endogamous groups. This has led Mandelbaum (1970) to identify *jāti* with *sub-caste* and *jāti cluster* with *caste*; while Klass (1980: 92-104; 178-81) regards the marriage-circle, an endogamous group having geographical boundaries and the power of expulsion, as the effective unit of the caste system and even the key to its origin. Exactly which groups should be called castes, sub-castes, jātis or marriage-circles does not affect the argument here; what concerns us is the contrast between all these and varṇa.

Though the number and ranking order of jātis is fluid, there seems to be a general recognition in all regions of two distinct groups of jātis at the top and bottom of the hierarchy. At the top are the brahmins. At the bottom are those jātis which have been variously called 'untouchable' (aspṛśya), 'ex-untouchable' (as if what was declared illegal in the 1949 constitution no longer existed), 'exterior castes', 'scheduled castes' (an official term established by the Government of India Act, 1935), or, following Gandhi, 'Harijans'. In what follows I shall call them 'dalits' (Skt. *dalita* 'crushed, oppressed'), a name created by themselves, not handed down by hostile or well-meaning outsiders. According to the 1931 census (the last to yield relevant figures), brahmins were only 4.5% of the population of undivided India, and 6.4% of Hindus, despite their prominence in the political and intellectual life of the past three millennia. Dalits were 14.9% of the population and 21.1% of Hindus (Schwartzberg 1978: 106). In a given district there may be several brahmin jātis and several dalit jātis.

While *jāti* is a Sanskrit word, with cognates of similar meaning in other South Asian languages, it does not always have in those languages the precise meaning summarized above. Like words in other languages for hereditary groups of people—e.g. *family, kindred, nation, race*—it can refer to various wider and narrower groups in different contexts. A jāti in Sanskrit can be a lineage or a nation of people, a genus, species or breed of animals, or, as a technical term in logic, a class of things. The meaning summarized on p. 9 is the one current in specialist work in English on South Asian society; the restriction of the word to this sense is foreign to South Asian languages, but this sense, as one among many, is indigenous.

Though *varṇa*, like *jāti*, refers to a number of hereditary groups ranked hierarchically, it is a word of very different meaning. While there is an indefinite number of jātis, there are only four varṇas; 'There is no fifth' (*Manu* 10, 4). While the dalits are sometimes called the fifth (pañcama) group, they are not a varṇa but a group of jātis outside the varṇas (a-varṇa). The number of varṇas does not change with time, except for the earliest Vedic period where we read of two varṇas, the Āryas and the non-Āryas, Dāsas or Dasyus (e.g. *ṚV* 3, 34, 9; 2, 12, 4).

As well as the number, the ranking order of the varṇas is definite. Except for some Vedic texts where we find evidence of disputes over the relative position of brahmins and kṣatriyas (e.g. *BṛhUp* 1, 4, 11; cf. p. 3), and Buddhist texts where kṣatriyas are regularly ranked above brahmins, the order has remained unchanged and undisputed through time. It is also standard throughout South Asia, though as we shall see later, its relation to social realities varies.

There is thus a fundamental structural difference between the concept of jāti and that of varṇa. The varṇas constitute a closed set; that is, 'one of fixed, and usually small, membership' (Lyons 1968: 436). The jātis, on the other hand, constitute an open set, with 'unrestricted, indeterminately large, membership' (ibid.). With a closed set, the addition or omission of a member affects the structure of the whole. For instance, if the closed set of English personal pronouns were expanded by introducing a gender-free animate pronoun meaning 'he or she', the use of the existing pronouns would be radically affected. To take an actual example, the introduction of *Ms* as a title for women which does not specify marital status has affected the use of *Miss* and *Mrs* by adding a third to a closed set of two. Such changes rarely occur; on the other hand, changes in an open set such as that of nouns happen all the time without attracting notice. In the same way, the closed set of varṇas remains constant, while the open set of jātis can and does change frequently.

Another fundamental difference is that the existence of a jāti, its characteristics, and its relationship with other jātis are established through the observation of South Asian society. The authority for the existence of the varṇas, on the other hand, lies in a textual tradition which can be traced to the myth of the primaeval man in the Vedic hymn known as the Puruṣa-sūkta ('hymn of the Man'):

> The brahmin was his mouth; his arms were made the prince (rājanya); his thighs were the vaiśya; from his feet the śūdra was born (*ṚV* 10, 90, 12).[2]

This hymn does not use the word *varṇa*, but already in later Vedic literature this word is associated with the four-term system:

> for there are four varṇas: brahmin, rājanya, vaiśya, śūdra (*ŚBr* 5, 5, 4, 9).[3]

The system of four varṇas is a topic which recurs throughout the literature of dharma, and the Puruṣa-sūkta is often quoted or alluded to in connection with it. The association of the four varṇas with parts of the body of the primaeval man is interpreted—as was no doubt intended—as showing their ranking order. These parts of the body also correspond to the functions of the varṇas: the brahmin, as speaker of the Veda and eater of offerings, comes from the mouth; the kṣatriya, as fighter and protector, from the arms; and the śūdra, as supporter of the body and main recipient of pollution, from the feet. The thighs suggest labour and perhaps also fertility.

A final difference between jāti and varṇa is that, while varṇa is a Hindu concept, resting on the authority of the Veda and the brahmins, jāti is observable throughout South Asian society, not only among Hindus but among Muslims and Christians.

So far we have discussed varṇa as if the traditional accounts of it were uniform, but this is a simplification. While the system of four varṇas is a recurrent topic from the Puruṣa-sūkta to the Purāṇas and later, there are many texts in which the only real distinction is

2 brāhmaṇo 'sya mukham āsīd bāhū rājanyaḥ kṛtaḥ / ūrū tad asya yad vaiśyaḥ padbhyāṃ śūdro ajāyata. *pad*, conventionally translated 'foot', refers also to the lower leg; cf. p. 3.

3 catvāro vai varṇāh. brāhmaṇo rājanyo vaiśyah śūdro...
There is some variation in the Brāhmaṇa texts (Macdonell and Keith 1912: II, 252) between *brahman* and *brāhmaṇa*; *rājan*, *rājanya* and *kṣatriya*; *viśya*, *vaiśya* and *ārya* (meaning here an Āryan commoner as distinct from the brāhmaṇa and kṣatriya who are the Āryan ruling classes). Besides the above masculine nouns denoting men of the first three varṇas, and the corresponding feminine nouns, there are *brahman* (n), *kṣatra* (n) and *viś* (f) which denote their respective statuses or functions.

between brahmins and non-brahmins. In the commentaries on *Manu*, for instance, the term *dvija* 'twice-born', which is stated in *Manu* 10, 4 to comprise brahmins, kṣatriyas and vaiśyas, is repeatedly glossed as referring to brahmins only; the same gloss is given for its synonym *ārya*. This suggests that between the compilation of *Manu* (2nd century CE?) and the time of the commentators the kṣatriya and vaiśya varṇas ceased to be recognized, leaving two varṇas only; the discrepancy between this and the four-varṇa system could be accounted for by the fact that this is the Kali age. The tradition also varies geographically; in Gujarat, for instance, Sanskrit texts speak of a polarity of brahmin and vaiśya which is not usual elsewhere (Das 1977).

Moreover, the distinction between brahmins and non-brahmins is described according to two conflicting principles: one hereditary, and the other qualitative. Generally in the dharma literature the hereditary principle prevails: the son of brahmin parents is a brahmin, and the son of śūdra parents is a śūdra (*Manu* 10, 5). According to this principle,

> Ill-behaved brahmins are to be honoured, and not śūdras who control their faculties; as cows that eat what they should not are honoured, and not well-disposed pigs.[4]

According to the qualitative principle, however, only those who behave as brahmins are brahmins. Not only can a brahmin by breach of his dharma become a śūdra or a vaiśya (*Manu* 10, 92-3), but Viśvāmitra and other mythical figures are known to have become brahmins through the power of tapas (asceticism). Even Manu says that an unlearned brahmin is a brahmin in name only, like a leather deer or a wooden elephant (*Manu* 2, 157). In the *MBh* and elsewhere we find many verses claiming that varṇa, particularly that of the brahmin, is determined by quality and not by birth.

> Truth, generosity, patience, good conduct, harmlessness, tapas, compassion: where this is found, that man is said to be a brahmin (*MBh* 3, 180, 21).

> Not birth, not initiation, not Veda-knowledge, not even lineage cause a person to be twice-born; the only cause is behaviour (*MBh* 13, 143, 50).

The application of this principle is exemplified in the *VajUp (Vajrasūcī Upaniṣad)*, whose use by Rammohun Roy we shall notice later (p. 20). When seen in the context of ancient Indian discourse, the qualitative principle does not necessarily undermine the hereditary one. For one thing, this is the Kali age, when not all the principles of dharma are applicable; for another, it is a well-established principle of interpretation that disparagement of something (in this case the unworthy brahmin) is intended not in its literal sense, but

4 anācārā dvijāḥ pūjyā na ca śūdrā jitendriyāḥ / abhakṣya-bhakṣakā gāvaḥ kolāḥ sumatayo na ca. *Padma Purāṇa*, quoted in Banerjea (1851).

as exaltation of something else (in this case, the qualities proper to a brahmin).[5] Nevertheless, the availability of the qualitative principle was vital for the development in the nineteenth century of a new understanding of varṇa, as we shall see.

The relationship between varṇa and jāti

Since the textual tradition is not insulated from social and historical realities, jāti has influenced the concept of varṇa. In post-Vedic times, Sanskrit writers have attempted to account for the hundreds of jātis by reference to the four varṇas. The literature of dharma from *Manu* onwards abounds in passages in which particular jātis are said to be descended either from miscegenation between the varṇas (e.g. *Manu* 10, 8-19; 25-39), or from members of particular varṇas who lapsed from their proper dharma (*Manu* 10, 20-3; 43-4). Such explanations vary between different dharma books, and have no historical value; we cannot suppose, for instance, that all Vaidehas are descended from kṣatriya fathers and brahmin mothers (*Manu* 10, 11) rather than from men and women of Videha. The explanations represent an attempt to relate the complexities of society at the time of the authors to the norms established in the Veda. In accordance with the standard doctrine that we are now in the Kali age, and have been since 3,102 BCE, the complexities of jāti are seen as a sign of degeneracy. Varṇa-saṃkara, 'mixture of varṇas', is prominent among the disasters predicted by Arjuna as a consequence of the great battle which he faces (*BhG* 1, 41-3). This battle took place at the beginning of the Kali age.

The desire to relate present realities to Vedic or other textual norms is found in many fields of Sanskrit learning at various periods. The post-Vedic practice of building temples, for instance, is related to Vedic ritual by using Vedic terms such as *vedi* for parts of the temple, and by speaking of the founder of the temple as a *yajamāna*—literally, the patron and beneficiary of a Vedic sacrifice. The rewards accruing to him are said to be equal to those resulting from Vedic ritual:

> He who wishes to enter the worlds that are entered by iṣṭāpūrta should build a temple to the gods; by doing so he attains the results of both iṣṭa and āpūrta (*Bṛhat-Saṃhitā* 55, 2).

Vedic mantras are quoted in connection with rituals and myths which developed later than the Veda, and post-Vedic texts are said to

5 na hi nindā nindyaṃ ninditum prayujyate. kim tarhi? ninditād itarat praśaṃsitum. tatra na ninditasya pratiṣedho gamyate kim tv itarasya vidhiḥ. 'The purpose of disparagement is not to disparage the thing disparaged. What is it, then? To praise what is other than the thing disparaged. It implies not a prohibition of what is disparaged, but an injunction to do something else.' Śabarasvāmin on *Jaiminīya-Sūtra* 2, 4, 20.

derive their authority and sanctity from the Veda.[6] The reinterpretations of Vedic texts and concepts by Dayānanda Sarasvatī and others in modern times are of the same kind; they should be seen not as distortions of history or as misinterpretations of scripture, but as attempts to ensure that the world is a realization of a sacred pattern, and not the result of an autonomous, and therefore wholly profane, series of events. They are also attempts to maintain the view that the Veda is the source of all knowledge and a blueprint for the universe.

Non-Vedic texts can similarly influence the ways in which present realities are understood. For instance, texts give a list of four Vaiṣṇava saṃpradāyas or sects: those of Rāmānuja, Madhva, Nimbārka and Viṣṇusvāmin (Entwistle 1987: 8-9). This is not a list that one would arrive at by observing the sects that exist today. The present-day reality is related to it by regarding existing sects as derived from those in the list: the Caitanya sect from Madhva, and the Vallabha saṃpradāya or Puṣṭi Mārga from the obscure Viṣṇusvāmin.

While the accounts of the derivation of the jātis from the varṇas are plainly unhistorical, they are partly based on principles which still apply in South Asian society. They show a preference for hypergamous (anuloma) unions over hypogamous (pratiloma) ones, and hypergamy is practised between subdivisions of certain jātis, and even in some regions between certain jātis (Tambiah 1973: 218-23). Some of the low jātis to which the law-books ascribe twice-born ancestors may themselves have claimed such ancestry, as many jātis do today (Tambiah 1973: 208). The theory that certain formerly kṣatriya jātis have lapsed to the position of śūdras through failure to practise their dharma is applied to people in remote parts of South Asia such as the Tamils, or outside it, such as the Greeks, Scythians and Chinese (*Manu* 10, 43-4), whom the people among whom the text was composed would have known principally as powerful rulers or as enemies in war. The theory recognized them as kṣatriyas de facto, while denying that they were kṣatriyas de jure. Further, in reading accounts of the jātis in the dharma texts we experience some uncertainty as to whether each jāti occupies a position within a particular varṇa, or an interstice between two varṇas, as appears from the phrase 'the dharmas of all the varṇas and of those born in between them' (*Manu* 1, 2).[7] Such uncertainty matches the uncertainty which faces any attempt to assign the jātis of present-day South Asia to particular varṇas.

The existence of an indefinite number of jātis competing with one another for places in the hierarchy was recognized by the dharma writers by means of the topics of jāty-utkarṣa and jāty-apakarṣa—the

6 E.g.: 'The Epics, Purāṇas and Dharma-śāstra have come into existence in order to reveal the meritorious acts prescribed in the Vedas. The benefits that can be had through reading the Vedas can also be had through reading the Epics and Purāṇas...Some Sahasra-nāmas are similarly praised as very excellent by great people' (*Vaidika dharma varttinī*, a Madras brahmin magazine, quoted by Diehl (1956: 89). See also Renou (1960).

7 sarva-varṇānām...antara-prabhavānām ca dharmān.

raising and lowering of jātis on the varṇa scale. Rules were devised whereby a jāti could come to occupy a higher or lower place on the scale than hitherto, though such rules vary greatly between different authorities (Kane 1941: 61-6).

While the social theories found in Sanskrit literature have been influenced by the facts of South Asian society, the social facts have in turn been influenced by the theories. Jātis adjust their ritual behaviour to the rules laid down in the śāstras for the varṇas to which they claim to belong; this can be seen in the different periods of impurity after a death (p. 79). The varṇa theory provides a reference model by which the status of a hitherto unknown jāti can be understood (Mandelbaum 1970: I, 24). It also provides a scale on which jātis can claim a place in an attempt to raise their status. Jātis whose neighbours regard them as śūdra may claim, sometimes in a quite explicit and organized way, to belong to one of the twice-born varṇas. The examples best known to history are jātis which have achieved royal status and therefore claim to be kṣatriya. Jātis with commercial occupations make similar claims to be vaiśyas, and craft jātis sometimes claim to be brahmins, such as the South Indian smiths who call themselves Viśvakarma brahmins (Srinivas 1962: 69), or the Yogīs, a Bengali weaving jāti (Bose 1959: 199f). This claim implies that the transmission of skills and knowledge required for the craft is of the same nature as the transmission of Vedic and other knowledge by the brahmins.

Such claims are unlikely to be accepted by all. Would-be kṣatriyas have to contend with the myth of Paraśurāma, who exterminated the kṣatriyas in the Tretā Yuga; many texts state that there are no true kṣatriyas in the Kali Yuga, and some also deny that there are any true vaiśyas. On the other hand, the myth of Paraśurāma can be used to support apparently extravagant claims: a jāti of potters or oil-pressers, for instance, may claim kṣatriya status by making its own version of the myth, in which its kṣatriya ancestors escaped the massacre by disguising themselves as potters or oil-pressers as the case might be (Mayer 1960: 62). Such claims, however, are unlikely to convince those outside the jāti; in these cases the function of the varṇa theory is to provide the jāti with a view of itself, rather than to influence the views of others.

The varṇa model explains some apparent anomalies in the ranking of jātis. If the acceptance of food were the sole criterion for jāti ranking, we should expect meat-eating jātis to rank below vegetarian ones. This is often the case; but on the other hand a jāti which claims to be kṣatriya and which eats meat, a diet considered appropriate for kṣatriyas, may rank above a vegetarian jāti (Mayer 1960: 39; Dumont 1972: 114; 128). This can be explained by the superiority of kṣatriyas to vaiśyas and śūdras.

The boundary in the varṇa system which corresponds most closely to a relatively undisputed boundary among the jātis is that between brahmin and non-brahmin; in other words, the kind of claim to a place on the varṇa scale that is most likely to be accepted or rejected unanimously by other jātis is the claim to be brahmin. Nevertheless, some jātis which claim brahmin status, such as the smiths mentioned above, are generally not accepted as such by others. The boundary between śūdras and the fifth group—the pañcamas, avarṇas, untouchables or dalits—also corresponds to a social reality, although the boundary dividing the untouchables from the others is not an undisputed one. Not only do some jātis try to reject untouchable status, but some try to claim it, in order to avail themselves of the positive discrimination provided in modern India for what are officially called scheduled castes. The boundary between śūdra and the non-brahmin twice-born varṇas—kṣatriyas and vaiśyas—is very fluid, in that many jātis claim kṣatriya or vaiśya status which are considered sūdras by their neighbours. The distinction in the dharma literature between dvijas or twice-born, who are entitled to wear the sacred thread, and the śūdras, who are not, is of little practical value, since some jātis have a sacred thread who would not be entitled to it according to the literature (Babb 1975: 79; cf p. 75 below).

It has often been pointed out that in South India the kṣatriya and vaiśya varṇas correspond to no social reality, since every jāti that is not brahmin is śūdra (Dumont 1972: 112). The same is sometimes said of Bengal (Sarma 1980: 10; 109), and even of India as a whole (Irving 1853: 16). While in other regions there are many jātis claiming vaiśya or kṣatriya status, we have seen that according to the dharma literature the kṣatriya category, and perhaps also the vaiśya, is empty in the Kali Yuga. Moreover, the varṇa system is not necessarily used as a criterion for the ranking of a jāti. The Vaidyas of Bengal, for instance, whose traditional occupation is medicine, rank next to brahmins, and some of them wear the sacred thread. However, this ranking does not seem to depend on any claim to be kṣatriyas, although the Sen kings of Bengal belonged to this jāti; rather, the Vaidyas sometimes claim to be brahmins, which is not only appropriate to an occupation that depends on inherited skill and knowledge, but is also the only way they can claim twice-born status if the only varṇas admitted to exist in Bengal are brahmins and śūdras. The myth of origin given for them in the *SkP* is an elaboration of Manu's statement that an Ambaṣṭha, whose occupation is medicine, has a brahmin father and a vaiśya mother (*Manu* 10, 8; Risley 1891: I, 46). The Vaidyas claim to rank above the Kāyasthas, who according to the *SkP* are descended from a kṣatriya child who was spared by Paraśurāma on condition that he was raised as a śūdra (Risley 1891: I, 438); the Kāyasthas for their part claim to be kṣatriyas and therefore superior to the Vaidyas. In such a situation the ranking of jātis depends on local traditions rather than on the all-India tradition of varṇa.

Sanskrit literature is not entirely consistent in its use of the words *jāti* and *varṇa*. In *Manu* 10, 27 and 31, for instance, *varṇa* appears where *jāti* must be meant; and in *Manu* 3, 15; 8, 177 and 9, 86-7 probably, and *Manu* 10, 41 certainly, *jāti*, which as we have seen is a word of wide meaning, is used in the sense of *varṇa* (cf. Kane 1962: 1633). Again, in the early nineteenth-century Sanskrit encyclopaedia *Śabda-kalpadruma* (Deb 1967), the entry on the word *jāti* is concerned with the four varṇas as well as with species of animals, while the entry on *varṇa* glosses this word as *jāti* before enumerating the four varṇas and describing their mythical origin and their duties.

Nevertheless, these are only occasional departures from the distinctive use of the two terms, and even where the two concepts are not expressly distinguished, the structural difference between them ensures that it is usually clear which of them is meant.

In English, though the distinction between the concepts has often been pointed out, the word *caste* is often used for both. The Portuguese word *casta* from which it is derived, meaning 'species, breed, lineage', is known from the sixteenth century in the sense of *jāti* (examples in Yule & Burnell 1903: 171), and passed into English soon afterwards. Until the nineteenth century it was usually spelt *cast*, and was 'app[arently] often assumed to be merely a particular application of' (*OED:* s.v. *caste*) the noun *cast* in the sense 'type, sort', as in *cast of mind, cast of countenance*. (Indeed, the Portuguese word may be Germanic in origin and cognate with *cast,* and not derived from Latin *castus* 'chaste' as commonly supposed (Pitt-Rivers 1971: 234).) It was used in a wider range of senses than at present, overlapping with 'race', 'tribe' and 'nation', not necessarily with reference to India. With the growth of writing on India from the late eighteenth century it became more usually thought of as a peculiarly Indian term, but at the same time, as Sanskrit literature became increasingly known, and regarded as the key to knowledge of Indian culture, *caste* came to stand not only for jāti but also for varṇa, and varṇa was thought of as the origin of jāti. It is interesting that Colebrooke (1798), in an essay based on Sanskrit texts listing the jātis, speaks not of 'castes' but of 'classes', and sometimes, without clear distinction, 'tribes'; *caste* was evidently not yet established as the proper term for the Indian phenomenon. *Class* remained in use by the British in India throughout the nineteenth century and much of the twentieth (e.g. Killingley 1990: 12), as a term for jāti, or for a group of jātis regarded for official purposes as one 'class'. The term *depressed classes* was first officially used in 1916 for what were later called *scheduled castes* (Sarma 1980: 27)—that is, the large group of jātis which are now called *dalit*.

Dalits have sometimes also been called *outcastes*, which, through the homophony of *caste* with the perfect participle of the verb *cast,* invites confusion with those who have been 'cast out' from their caste, or 'outcasted', for breaches of purity.[8] This, together with their position outside the four varṇas, has led to a frequent misstatement that they belong to no caste. This misconception is reinforced by the long-established but confusing phrase 'caste Hindu', meaning a Hindu belonging to a non-dalit jāti. Because dalits are wrongly thought to be outside the caste system, their actual division into jātis is sometimes said to be not really caste but only an imitation of it (e.g. Isaacs 1965: 29).

As mentioned above (p. 11), jāti is a feature of South Asian

8 Indeed, Crooke (1917: 581b) speaks of these two categories as 'two classes' of 'outcastes', rather than as the referents of two homophonous words *outcaste* and *outcast*.

society in general, and not peculiar to Hindus. Nevertheless, perhaps because varṇa and jāti have been confused in the single term *caste*, caste is often thought of as a Hindu institution. One consequence of this has been the defence of caste by Hindu apologists, which will be described below (pp. 28-31). Another has been that when legislation to protect dalits was drafted, both in British India and in independent India, it excluded those who were not Hindu, on the assumption that

> an Untouchable who converts openly to Christianity, Buddhism or Islam ceases thereby to be an Untouchable (and therefore to be a member of a Scheduled Caste) even though the majority continues to discriminate against him as before (Dushkin 1972: 168).

The laws in question have since been amended to cover Buddhist dalits, but still exclude those who are converted to other religions.

Brāhmos and Christians in nineteenth-century Bengal

What came to be known in the course of the nineteenth century as social reform cannot be understood by simply contrasting the actual state of society at the time with some ideal form of society. The agenda for social reform was set by a complex process involving the ways in which South Asian society was understood by the reformers, and the forms of society which they regarded as ideal. Both in their understanding of society and in their ideals, the reformers were influenced by Western thought: by the Enlightenment, evangelicalism, utilitarianism and liberalism in the early part of the century, and later by Victorian ideas of progress, and by Comtean Positivism and its British offshoots. Their knowledge of South Asian society depended largely on a growing body of published research, by Westerners and South Asians, which itself was influenced by these schools of thought. This does not mean, however, that the reformers merely took up Western ideas; they contributed their own thought, drawing on South Asian and other sources.

One of the topics of social reform was the group of phenomena referred to as *caste*. We will sometimes be obliged to use this word to refer to what was treated at the time as a single topic, embracing hereditary grouping into jātis, jāti endogamy, rules of purity, hereditary occupations, and the dharmaśāstra theory of varṇa.

In the nineteenth century, the topic of caste did not figure so prominently on the agenda as that of women. This is not the place to discuss the reasons for the prominence of women as a topic in social reform. We may, however, reflect on Vivekānanda's judgment that this topic tended to eclipse others, including that of caste:

> All that you mean by your social reform is either widow remarriage, or female emancipation, or something of that sort...And again these are directed within the confines of a few of the castes only (Vivekānanda, conversation, 22.1.1898: V, 333).

When caste was discussed, the aspects of it which were most apparent were its divisiveness and the requirements of ritual purity, transgression of which was called 'loss of caste' or 'breach of caste' (jāti-dhvaṃsa, jāti-bhraṃśa). The need to avoid such transgression affects the higher jātis more severely than the lower, and is a frequent target of early nineteenth-century discourse on caste. The disabilities of the lower jātis did not figure on the agenda until late in the nineteenth century, largely because the reformers belonged to the higher jātis: in Bengal, brahmins, Vaidyas and Kāyasthas. Since these three did not differ greatly in prestige and power, the divisions between jātis may have been more apparent to the reformers than their inequality.

Rammohun Roy does not often refer to caste in his English works; when he does, it is to 'our division into castes, which has been the source of want of unity among us' (Rammohun, preface to *Brahmunical Magazine:* II, 138). This want of unity he sees as an obstacle to political development:

> I regret to say that the present system of religion adhered to by the Hindus is not well calculated to promote their political interest. The distinction of castes introducing innumerable divisions and sub-divisions among them has entirely deprived them of patriotic feeling, and the multitude of religious rites and ceremonies and the laws of purification have totally disqualified them from undertaking any difficult enterprise (Rammohun, letter of 18.1.1828: IV, 95).

In these quotations what Rammohun means by *caste* is clearly jāti, not varṇa. He does not usually refer to varṇa in his English works. In the last paragraph of his *Second Conference on the Practice of Burning Widows Alive,* he mentions 'Brahmans, or those of other tribes' (Rammohun: III, 126); here the word *tribe* translates Bengali *varṇa* (Rāmamohana: III, 47). A few lines later he uses the word *tribe* again; this time it translates *jāti,* but in the sense of 'nation', not in the sense that concerns us here. Since he does not give a clear translation of the word *varṇa* here, he does not seem to expect his European readers to be interested in the concept. Elsewhere, however, in a technical discussion in which the concept of varṇa is important, he speaks of the four 'classes' (Rammohun, *Apology:* II, 124). Here, he argues that entitlement to 'divine knowledge' (brahma-vidyā) is independent of varṇa; he claims Śaṅkara's authority for this view, incidentally ignoring the contrary statement in Śaṅkara's commentary on *VS* 1, 3, 34, which he accepts without question in his own Bengali commentary on the same sūtra.

Rammohun also refers to 'what is commonly called loss of caste', which he explains as 'exclusion from the society of his family and friends', which a Hindu is liable to suffer for breaking a rule of diet (Rammohun, introduction to *ĪśUp:* II, 51). He deplores such rules. However, he was careful not to break caste in his own life, wearing the sacred thread and taking a brahmin cook with him to England; and in the Brāhmo Samāj he gave brahmins their traditional role as readers and expounders of the Vedas. This is consistent with Rammohun's view of Hindu society. He objected to the divisive effect of jāti, and held that all should have equal opportunity to know God, but he did not consider that all should be socially equal.

It has sometimes been pointed out that Rammohun opposed caste by publishing and translating a Sanskrit text, the *VajUp,* in 1827. This is an Advaita text of unknown date, which attacks the idea that one can be a brahmin by birth; its ideas are similar to those of a Buddhist text, also called *Vajrasūcī* (Mukhopadhyaya 1960; Killingley 1977: 298-326). The *VajUp* exists in several recensions; the one used by Rammohun concludes:

> Therefore the knower of Brahman, and no-one else, is a brahmin...By a greater or lesser degree of that knowledge one is a kṣatriya or a vaiśya; by lack of it, a śūdra (Rāmamohana: IV, 45-6).

The work criticizes the concept of varṇa, not that of jāti. In doing so, it does not mean to undermine the position of brahmins; its aim is to exalt the knower of Brahman. It presents standard Advaita Vedānta doctrine, saying that the distinctions between brahmin and non-brahmin, like all distinctions, have no ultimate value (Killingley 1977: 305f; 310). To anyone familiar with Advaita, this does not mean that such distinctions have no value for worldly purposes.

Neither varṇa nor jāti is a frequent topic in Rammohun's works. When they do occur, they are kept apart; varṇa is used in arguments with Hindu opponents, where Rammohun regularly uses traditional śāstric ideas, while jāti is referred to in his criticisms of Hindu social practices. Unlike some of the later writers whose ideas we shall examine, he does not use varṇa in apologetic; in the two works in which he writes under pseudonyms as an advocate for Hinduism against Christianity, the *Brahmunical Magazine* and the Ram Doss letters, the topics of varṇa and jāti do not appear.

After Rammohun Roy, many Bengalis took up more radical attitudes to caste. From the 1830s, the amorphous class of English-educated young men known as Young Bengal deliberately flouted rules of ritual purity, while the issue of jāti division, and especially the division between the brahmins and the other jātis, was a frequent topic of debate in the Brāhmo Samāj. The question of whether brahmins in the Samāj should wear the sacred thread, and whether non-brahmins could be ācāryas ('ministers' in the Samāj's English terminology), led to the first schism in the Samāj in 1865.

In 1851 an article on 'Hindu caste' appeared in the *Calcutta Review* (Banerjea 1851). It is anonymous, but generally attributed to Krishna Mohan Banerjea, a member of Young Bengal who became a Christian under the influence of Alexander Duff in 1832 (De 1962: 586n). Like many earlier writers he uses the words *order, class, tribe, race* and *caste* interchangeably, though he prefers *caste* as a term for the institution as a whole, which is 'different from that of any other country' (Banerjea 1851: 37). He does not explicitly distinguish varṇa from jāti. He does, however, address the contemporary situation, particularly in Bengal, and attempts to relate it to the śāstras. He sees the varṇas as the origin of the jātis, and accepts the theory of 'mixed races' as historical.

He roundly condemns caste: it 'exercises a baneful influence on the development of the human mind' by restricting occupations (Banerjea 1851: 66). 'It really injures the Brahmin no less than the Sudra, by compelling both to adopt professions, which may be opposed to their tastes', and by keeping brahmins from gainful occupations (Banerjea 1851: 71). But he sees the multiplicity of jātis not as a falling away from an ideal original system of varṇa, but as the outcome of faults inherent in that system.

> That the countless ramifications of the servile classes are monstrous corruptions of the original division, can admit of no doubt. But there was something in the Hindu institution of caste [i.e. varṇa] which was naturally liable to corruption. It was fit for no other than *monstrous* growth (Banerjea 1851: 37).

The varṇa system was set up by the brahmins for their own benefit. Its myth of origin, as given in *RV* 10, 90, is 'blasphemy' and a 'spiritual forgery' (Banerjea 1851: 75). Like Dayānanda after him, he compares the brahmins to popes, seeing the latter through Protestant eyes.

Banerjea is aware of the discrepancies between the varṇa model and the facts of jāti in Bengal.

> The Vaishyas and Sudras, as pure orders, are extinct at least in Bengal. The Kshetriyas are scarce. The dignity of the twice-born is almost monopolized by Brahmins (Banerjea 1851: 62).

By the extinction of śūdras he seems to mean that they do not exist as a jāti distinct from the 'mixed' jātis. He notes that the Vaidyas and Kāyasthas rank next to brahmins, and even finds that they have an ascendancy over them. For instance, 'the President of the Dharma Sobha of Calcutta [Rādhākānta Deb] is a Kayastha and Sudra, while the Secretary [Bhawānīcharaṇ Bannerji] is a Brahmin.' The main features of caste which he notes are the dominance of brahmins 'in matters spiritual', the high position of Vaidyas, Kāyasthas and the group of nine jātis called navaśākhā, endogamy and commensality, and kulīnism (Banerjea 1851: 63).

Despite his awareness of the Bengali situation, Banerjea still sometimes uses the terminology of varṇa. To exemplify the 'baneful influence' of occupational restrictions, he writes:

> The Brahmin or the Kshetriya may have a son, whose mind is ill adapted to his hereditary profession. The Vaishya may have a son with a natural dislike for a counting-house, and the Sudra may have talents superior to his birth.

Here, his general critique of the tradition is expressed in more traditional terms than is his more precise account of the Bengali situation.

A somewhat similar account of caste was given by Śivanāth Śāstrī, the leader of the Sādhāraṇ Brāhmo Samāj, in his Bengali lecture *Jātibhed* ('jati division') in 1884. He accepts the traditional origin of jāti in the four varṇas, and combines it with the modern historical theory of the Āryan invasion. The brahmins were appointed to preserve the mantras, which were (as in Max Müller's widely accepted view) the spontaneous nature-poetry of the Āryans. The kṣatriyas were established to protect the Āryans from the indigenous Dasyus, and the remaining Āryans were the viś. Those non-Āryans who submitted to Āryan rule became the śūdras.

This original system of varṇa, then, served a useful function in the Vedic period. It was free from the features which Śāstrī finds most objectionable in the jāti system: hereditary occupation, which deprives labour of dignity and encourages brahmins to beg; endogamy, which weakens the people genetically; and the prohibition of interdining. In the original system there was no 'allotment of particular occupations to particular castes'. This makes sense only if by *castes* we understand 'jātis', not 'varṇas'; the basis of the brahmin and kṣatriya varṇas was occupational in Śāstrī's view, but it seems that membership of them was not hereditary. As to the present system, Śāstrī is in no doubt that it is wholly evil and should be uprooted. Indeed, despite what he says about its present strength, he predicts its fall; it is already weakened by British rule, which has opened education to all, and made the śāstras available even to foreigners. While condemning the contemporary system of jāti, Śāstrī was thus able to justify varṇa, which he regarded as its historical origin.[9]

The Bengali Positivists and Hindu revivalism

Banerjea's and Śāstrī's adverse views of caste match those of many of their British contemporaries and predecessors. A much more favourable, though less well-informed, view of one aspect of caste was provided by Auguste Comte (1798-1857), the founder of Positivism.[10] Comte held that the brahmins constituted a class of priests and teachers who performed a similar function to the Catholic clergy in Europe (Forbes 1975: 9). He believed that they could be adapted to a new function as priests of his 'Religion of Humanity', in which theological doctrines would be replaced by scientific ones. This idea was taken up by Comte's English disciple Richard Congreve (1818-99), and passed by him to the leading Bengali advocate of Positivism, Jogendro Chandra Ghosh (1842-1902).

Jogendro developed his views on caste in a number of books and articles from 1873 onwards. He believed that social reform could only be brought about through the leadership of brahmins learned in the

9 I use the English translation (Śāstrī 1975), as I have not seen the original Bengali.

10 *Positivism* here is the name of the distinctive—indeed peculiar—set of doctrines promulgated by Comte, which while claiming to be based on reason are at many points arbitrary and idiosyncratic. The word *positivism* can be used in wider senses, but these are not intended here. Comtean Positivism and its propagation and reception in Bengal are discussed in Forbes (1975).

śāstras, since the brahmins were the natural guides of the śūdras. Besides this special position of the brahmins, the various śūdra jātis had their natural place in the hierarchy of Hindu society, providing united and disciplined occupational groups in which capital and labour were in the same hands. Reformed on Positivist principles, under the leadership of Positivist brahmins, the jāti system and the joint family would form the basis of a vigorous industrial society, free from the evils resulting from competition and from the exploitation of labour by capital. What Jogendro proposed to remove from the present system was its religious aspect, and its restrictions on sea voyage and on interdining between jātis (Forbes 1975: 87-9).

This favourable view of caste, in both its aspects of varṇa and jāti, was new among social reformers. It was, however, consistent with a trend which has been called Bengal Victorianism (Sinha 1965) or Hindu revivalism (Forbes 1975). In this trend, the violent break with tradition typical of Young Bengal is abandoned in favour of a version of traditional norms in which they are reinterpreted and adapted according to European ideals. Bhūdev Mukherjee (1827-98) is typical.

Bhūdev's career was devoted to education and to writing; he was the first Indian to become an Inspector of Schools (Mitra 1979: 82). He wrote a number of books in Bengali, in which he defended traditional Hindu social norms, while owing more than he was aware to Western values (Raychaudhuri 1988: 26-92). Like Jogendro, Bhūdev presented a favourable view of jāti as well as varṇa. In his *Sāmājika Prabandha* ('essay on society', 1898), he described the jātis as hereditary groups whose different dharmas avoided competition, and which together formed a harmonious society (Mitra 1979: 88-9). The dharmas of the different jātis corresponded to their inherited characteristics, which were of the same nature as racial differences. The foundation of the system was the four varṇas, which were immutable (Mitra 1979: 100).

Satish Chandra Mukherjee (1865-1948) was at first a Positivist but later became an associate of Vivekānanda, and was eventually initiated by the Vaiṣṇava guru and former Brāhmo, Bijoy Krishna Goswāmī (Forbes 1975: 127-8; 140). In articles published in his own monthly *Dawn* between 1900 and 1904, he envisaged a new spiritual and intellectual leadership which would replace the brahmins both as spiritual guides and as communicators of modern Western ideas. He does not say how this class would be chosen, but apparently it would not be hereditary (Forbes 1975: 142).

Under the influence of the Positivists, much of the discourse on caste in Bengal was concerned with the special position of brahmins, justifying it on the lines proposed by Comte. Since intellectual leadership in Bengal was shared among brahmins, Vaidyas and Kāyasthas, this concern suggests that the writers were looking at the theory of varṇa, as laid down in the śāstras or as reported in modern sources, rather than at the actual position of the jātis.

The Bengali novelist Bankim Chandra Chatterji (1838-94) was familiar with Comte's work but used it critically and selectively; he was a friend of the Positivist Jogendro Chandra Ghosh, and published Jogendro's Bengali article on Comte in his own Bengali journal *Baṅga Darśana* (Forbes 1975: 133). His Bengali treatise on religion, *DhT*

(*Dharma-tattva*, 'the essence of religion') is one of the most original attempts to reformulate Hinduism in the light of Western ideas (King 1977); he has been called a pioneer of neo-Hinduism (Antoine 1953). In this work, and also in his unfinished commentary on the *BhG*, Bankim detached the concept of varṇa from that of jāti in a similar way to Dayānanda (below, p. 27), passing a favourable judgment on the former while denouncing the latter. Bankim was aware of Dayānanda's views, though he objected to his attempt to restore past forms (Forbes 1975: 131). He was probably prompted by Dayānanda's revolutionary use of the concept of varṇa, but he developed this concept in his own way.

In 1879, in his book *Sāmya* ('equality'), Bankim had given an unfavourable view of varṇa. He says there that while inequality based on physical or mental differences is natural, inequality based on birth, as that between brahmin and śūdra, is unnatural. The gravest form of social inequality in the world is the inequality of varṇa founded on the Vedic dharma, from which the Buddha was the first to rescue India (Chatterji 1969: 382). Bankim condemns the distinction whereby the dust of a brahmin's feet is to be put on one's head, while a śūdra is untouchable (aspṛśya); this exaggerated description of the śūdra shows how little the real phenomenon of untouchability impinged on his consciousness. He analyses Indian society in terms of the four varṇas, condemning the restriction of learning to the brahmins as a hindrance to progress, and attributing decline to the poverty of the śūdras and their oppression by brahmins. He also devotes a chapter to sexual inequality, holding up Īshvar Chandra Vidyāsāgar, the champion of widow remarriage, as an example for other reformers to follow.

Towards the end of *Sāmya*, Bankim mentions a third form of inequality besides those of varṇa and sex, namely *jāti*. This word, however, he uses not in the sense of 'caste' but in that of 'race' or 'nation'. The inequality he is thinking of here is that between a conquering race or nation and the conquered, which he says is too well known to need discussion (Chatterji 1969: 406); he is clearly thinking of the inequality between the British and the Indians, which he had himself experienced as an uncovenanted civil servant. He does not apply the word *jāti* to the divisions within the Indian population. He does, however, show that he is aware that this word can have the sense of 'caste', since he says in passing that what he refers to here as *jāti* is not the same as the varṇa distinctions of ancient India.

Bankim here adds this book's last word on varṇa. While varṇa causes the social inequality described earlier, at the present time it does not, he says, cause inequality of adhikāra 'entitlement'. This word presumably refers here to civil or legal rights, not to entitlement to perform particular rituals or to have them performed.[11] He therefore thinks of varṇa as a form of social classification which is essentially harmful, but no longer as harmful in modern times as formerly.

A very different view of varṇa is seen in the two works already mentioned which Bankim wrote towards the end of his life, *DhT*,

11 Haldar (1974) translates *adhikāragata vaiṣamya* here as 'diversity of rights'.

and his unfinished commentary on the *BhG*.

In *DhT*, Bankim does not deal with varṇa in general, but with the special case of the brahmins. These he saw as Comte saw them, as lawgivers and teachers who were honoured above kings (Chatterji 1969: 617; tr. Ghose 1977: 68). For this reason they are the highest varṇa, and objects of devotion (bhakti) for all. Moreover, though they were lawgivers, they did not appropriate wealth to themselves; on the contrary, they debarred themselves from kingship, trade and agriculture, and were content to live on gifts. They did, however, also ordain that devotion was due to them, because that is necessary if a pupil is to learn from a teacher.

Bankim locates this Comtean ideal of the brahmin in an unspecified period of the past. Turning to the popular notion of the greedy, venal and ignorant brahmin of his own time, he asks:

> When brahmins lost those qualities which made them worthy of it, why did we still give them our devotion? (Chatterji 1969: 618).

Today, devotion to brahmins is still a duty, but should be given to a different class of people.

> We shall be devoted to him who has the qualities of a brahmin — that is, who is righteous, learned, free from desire and a teacher of the people — and not to someone who lacks them.

Bankim thus puts forward a qualitative, non-hereditary view of varṇa, and of the brahmin in particular. He then considers how this is related to jāti. Brahmins, he notes, were pupils of Keshub Chunder Sen, who was a Vaidya.

> Indeed, that great man was graced with all the qualities of a true brahmin. He was worthy of all the devotion due to a brahmin.[12]

To provide traditional justification for his view, Bankim quotes ślokas from the *MBh* and the *Gautamīya-Saṃhitā* which describe brahminhood according to the qualitative principle.[13]

The same theme occurs in his commentary on *BhG* 4, 13, where he again quotes the ślokas just mentioned, and denies that membership of the varṇas is hereditary. Here, he speaks at first of the four varṇas, as the *BhG* does; however, much of the ensuing discussion, like the passage in *DhT*, mentions only brahmins and śūdras, the categories relevant to the Bengali situation.

In the verse under discussion Kṛṣṇa says:

> The four-varṇa system was created by me, according to the distribution of guṇas and actions. Though I am the agent of it, know that I am the

12 The passage referring to Keshub is omitted in Ghose's translation.

13 *MBh* 3, 206, 11-12; 3, 178, 43 in the critical edition. The *Gautamīya-Saṃhitā* is a ritual text followed by the Nimbārka sect (Farquhar 1920: 240, 376).

changeless non-agent (*BhG* 4, 13).

Bankim begins by pointing out that this verse does not agree with the commonly-cited myth of the origin of the varṇas from the mouth, arms, thighs and feet of the primaeval man (*ṚV* 10, 90, 12). He rejects a literal interpretation of this myth, and cites other Vedic texts which give different accounts of the origin of the varṇas, or rather of the twice-born varṇas since they do not mention the śūdras: from the three vyāhṛtis or sacred words *bhūḥ, bhuvaḥ, svaḥ* (*ŚBr* 2, 1, 4, 11), or from the three Vedas (*TBr* 3, 12, 9, 2). There are many other examples, Bankim says, which he refrains from giving. Kṛṣṇa, he says, gives yet another view, in which varṇa is created by God according to the qualities (guṇa) and actions of each person. As these are formed after birth, varṇa is independent of lineage. It is in fact a way of classifying character (prakṛti):

> How does this difference in people's actions come about? It results from differences in their character. It is this difference of character that is the four-varṇa system, or difference of varṇa.[14]

It is caused by God not in the sense that he assigns varṇas individually, but because he is the ultimate agent of all action. This at least seems to be the point of the brief discussion of scientific laws with which Bankim ends his comment on this verse, saying that even if the world is held to operate according to laws, the establishment of these laws is itself an act of God.

Bankim also links varṇa closely with the topics of desireless action and salvation; this, he says, is why it is brought in at this point in the *BhG*. Only those who act desirelessly are entitled to salvation; Bankim uses here the ritualistic term *adhikāra* 'entitlement to perform a particular ritual', but he uses it in a non-ritualistic sense. By implication, those who act desirelessly are those whom the *BhG*, as interpreted by Bankim, calls brahmins, since brahmins are characterized by sattva which the *BhG* (e.g. *BhG* 18, 9) associates with desireless action.

Another passage from this commentary is repeated in an appendix to *DhT* (Chatterji 1969: 678-9; tr. Ghose 1977: 193-4). Here, Bankim gives a modified version of the varṇa system, justifying it on utilitarian lines rather than by an appeal to śāstra, and giving the brahmins, as the intellectual leaders of society, a special position which is thoroughly Comtean. First, he reduces the dharma of mankind to knowledge and action — a pair well established in the *BhG* and elsewhere — rejecting Comte's triad of thought, feeling and action. Knowledge, and above all knowledge of brahman, is the dharma of the brahmin. All action is related to objects of enjoyment or goods (bhogya), and is concerned with their production, collection and

14 loker madhye erūpa visadṛśa ācaraṇa deoẏā yāẏ kena? tāhādiger prakṛtibhedavaśataḥ. ei prakṛtibhedaī cāturvarṇya vā varṇabheda (Chatterji 1969: 772).

preservation. These three types of action are the dharmas of the śūdra, the vaiśya and the kṣatriya, namely agriculture, trade and warfare. Bankim admits that he has departed from tradition in making agriculture the dharma of the śūdra instead of one of the two functions of the vaiśya. But, he says, today the śūdras are mainly engaged in agriculture, as well as serving the other three varṇas; he might have added that today, in so far as vaiśyas are recognized at all, it is on the basis of their commercial, not their agricultural activities. He ends by listing five functions: acquisition of knowledge or teaching; warfare or the protection of society; crafts or commerce; production or agriculture; and service. This suggests that he envisages a fivefold varṇa system, but he does not carry the argument further.

Dayānanda Sarasvatī

The most revolutionary view of caste in the nineteenth century was that of Dayānanda Sarasvati (1824-83). Bankim was aware of Dayānanda, but considered him retrograde (Forbes 1975: 131); he may, however, have been inspired by Dayānanda's ideas on varṇa. These ideas were reported by Rudolf Hoernle, principal of Benares Sanskrit College, in 1870, in something very like their final form; unlike many of Dayānanda's ideas, therefore, they took shape well before his visit to Calcutta in 1872 (Jordens 1978: 62; 89).

Dayānanda, as a pandit learned in Sanskrit, used the traditional framework of varṇa. His view of it, however, is qualitative and not hereditary; he thus separates varṇa from jāti.

> Even now, he who has the best knowledge and nature is fit to be a brahmin, and a fool is fit to be a śūdra. And so it will be hereafter also (Dayānanda 1972a: 125; cf. 1972b: 83).[15]

He finds authority for this in *Manu* 2, 157 (p. 12), and 10, 65, which speaks of a śūdra becoming a brahmin and vice versa. He proposes that the qualitative principle should be put into practice.

> A place in the varṇa system according to qualities and actions should be fixed by examination, at the age of sixteen for a girl and at the age of twenty-five for a man (Dayānanda 1972a: 130; cf. 1972b: 87).[16]

For his reconstructed varṇas, Dayānanda upheld the principle of endogamy.

15 ab bhī jo uttama vidyā svabhāvavālā hai, bahī brāhmana ke yogya aur mūrkha śūdra ke yogya hotā hai. aur vaisā hī āge bhī hogā.

16 yah guṇa karmoṃ se varnoṃ kī vyavasthā kanyāoṃ kī solahaveṃ varṣa aur purusoṃ kī paccīsaveṃ varṣa kī parīkṣā meṃ niyata karaṇī cāhiye.

> Thus they will duly keep the actions of their own varṇas, as well as mutual love (Dayānanda, ibid.).[17]

He also prohibits interdining (Dayānanda 1972a: 400; 1972b: 263), though he allows the twice-born varṇas to employ śūdra cooks, provided strict hygiene is observed (Dayānanda 1972a: 392; 1972b: 259).

In his polemic against the Brāhmos, he condemns their rejection of jāti. However, he distinguishes here between two kinds of jāti: God-made and man-made. God-made jāti is species, of which human beings are one; man-made jāti is the division of people into brahmins, kṣatriyas, vaiśyas, śūdras and antyajas (untouchables).

> But among people, brahmin and so on are not ordinary jātis, but jātis of a special kind. As we said earlier in dealing with the system of varṇa and āśrama, varṇa must be considered as a matter of qualities, actions and natures. As these are man-made, it is the wish of the king and the learned to fix by examination the varṇas of brahmin, kṣatriya, vaiśya, śūdra, etc., as said before, according to their qualities, actions and nature (Dayānanda 1972a: 574; cf. 1972b: 373).[18]

The 'jātis of a special kind' are the varṇas. They are man-made in the sense that each person by his or her behaviour becomes fit for a particular varṇa, and in an ideal Āryan state would be assigned to it by a board of examiners. It is jāti in this special sense, namely varṇa, that Dayānanda accuses the Brāhmos of mistakenly rejecting (cf. Jordens 1978: 113).

Vivekānanda

Dayānanda's arguments are obscured by his occasional use of *jāti* in the sense of varṇa. This difficulty is more frequently found in literature in English, where the word *caste* is regularly used for both. Vivekānanda, most of whose works are in English, uses the same two revolutionary ideas as Dayānanda: that the four-varṇa system is the authentic form of caste, and that membership of a varṇa is to be determined on the qualitative principle. He makes little reference to the actual jātis; when he uses the word *caste*, he is often referring to varṇa.

Vivekānanda believes that caste is a natural order in society, and that it can be purified by abolishing caste privileges. This is part

17 tabhī āpne-āpne varnoṃ ke karma aur paraspara prīti bhī yathāyogya rahegī.

18 parantu manusyoṃ meṃ brāhmaṇādi ko sāmānya jāti meṃ nahīṃ, kintu sāmānyaviśeṣātmaka jāti mem nigate haim. jaise pūrva varṇāśramavyavasthā meṃ likh āye, vaise hī guṇa-karma-svabhāva se varṇavyavasthā mānanī avaśya hai. is manuṣyakṛtatva unke guṇa-karma-svabhāva se pūrvoktānusāra brāhmaṇa kṣatriya vaisya sūdrādi varnoṃ kī parīkṣāpūrvaka vyavasthā karaṇī rājā aur vidvānoṃ kā kāma hai.

of his general tendency to support Hinduism rather than oppose it, while calling at the same time for its reform.

> Wherever you go there will be caste. But that does not mean that there should be these privileges. They should be knocked on the head (Vivekānanda, 'Vedanta and Indian life': III, 245).

One such reform that he proposes is to replace the indefinite number of jātis with the four varṇas:

> We have to redivide the whole Hindu population, grouping it under the four main castes, of Brahmins, Kshatriyas, Vaishyas, and Shudras, as of old. The numberless modern subdivisions of the Brahmins that split them up into so many castes, as it were, have to be abolished and a single Brahmin caste to be made by uniting them all. Each of the three remaining castes also will have to be brought similarly into single groups, as was the case in Vedic times (Vivekānanda, 'Conversations XV': V, 405-6).

The words 'as it were' here imply that varṇa, not jāti, is the proper sense of the word *caste*.

Sometimes Vivekānanda denies that caste is a religious institution.

> The caste system is opposed to the religion of the Vedanta. Caste is a social custom, and all our great preachers have tried to break it down. From Buddhism downwards, every sect has preached against caste, and every time it has only riveted the chains. Caste is simply the outgrowth of the political institutions of India; it is a hereditry trade guild (Vivekānanda, speech in Boston, 1896: V, 311; cf. V, 22-3).

If we take *caste* in the sense of 'jāti' rather than 'varṇa' here, it is easier to understand why elsewhere Vivekānanda takes a different view of caste, as a spiritual order which is not hereditary. In justifying his initiating Westerners into the Veda by teaching them the praṇava (the syllable *Oṃ*), he says:

> My disciples are all Brahmins! I quite admit the truth of the words that none except the Brahmins has a right to the Pranava. But the son of a Brahmin is not necessarily a Brahmin; though there is every possibility of his being one, he may not become so...In India, one is held to be Brahmin because of one's caste, but in the West, one should be known as such by one's Brahmanya qualities (Vivekānanda, 'Conversations X': V, 376-7).

In the last sentence, where *caste* means 'jāti', Vivekānanda shows more caution than Dayānanda in the face of Hindu attitudes, by restricting the application of the qualitative principle to the West. But he distinguishes *caste* in the sense of 'jāti' from *true caste*, which is the spiritual hierarchy of varṇa.

> Buddha never fought true castes, for they are nothing but the congregation of those of a particular natural tendency, and they are always valuable. But Buddha fought the degenerated castes with their hereditary privileges, and

spoke to the Brahmins: '...Caste is a state, not an iron-bound class, and every one who knows and loves God is a true Brahmin' (Vivekānanda, speech in New York, 4.2.1895: II, 508).

This view, in which jāti is false caste, while varṇa, judged on a qualitative principle in which spiritual attainment rather than function in society is often the criterion, is true caste, has become standard in neo-Hinduism.[19] B. G. Tilak, in a speech at Kanpur in 1917, said:

Many of you now believe that *catur-varṇa* ['the four varṇas'] consists merely of different castes that divide us at present. No one thinks of the duties belonging to these castes...Bhagavadgita expressly states that this division was not by birth but by the quality and by the profession which were necessary to maintain the whole society in those days (Tilak 1922: 219).

BhG 18, 41-4 does indeed describe the qualities and functions of the varṇas, but does not deny the hereditary principle. Nevertheless, it is often asserted that it does; for instance, in an Indian law-suit 'the minority judgment referred to the *Gītā* for the theory that caste ultimately depended not on birth but on conduct: but this is not the accepted opinion' (Derrett 1968: 115n, citing *V. V. Giri* v. *D. Suri Dora, All IR* 1959 S.C. 1318).

Rādhākrishnan

Rādhākrishnan (1888-1975), like Vivekānanda, justifies caste before a Western audience by identifying true caste with a spiritual varṇa which is not hereditary.

The Hindu thinkers distinguish between the less evolved in whom the powers of self-analysis and self-direction have not arisen, and the more evolved or the twice-born who were graded into the three classes of Brahmin, Kṣatriya and Vaiśya. The different castes represent members at different stages on the road to self-realization. However lowly a man may be, he can raise himself sooner or later (Rādhākrishnan 1960: 85).

Later, addressing an Indian audience, he criticizes caste: 'The caste spirit must go'; it has become a 'system of false pride' (Rādhākrishnan 1947: 132). Though this has been seen as a turning away from his former justification of caste (Wadia 1952: 778), we may rather see it as a turning from caste as varṇa to caste as jāti. Rādhākrishnan has not abandoned his former view, for in the same pages he also describes the four varṇas, saying that 'caste divisions are based on individual temperament, which is not immutable' (Rādhākrishnan 1947: 129). The system of 'four orders' is 'a

19 For the term *neo-Hinduism*, see Antoine (1953); Hacker (1958).

classification based on social facts and psychology' (ibid. 130), and 'the basis of varṇa dharma is that every human being must try to fulfil the law of his development' (ibid. 131). Here Rādhākrishnan adapts the neo-Hindu interpretation of varṇa to his own insistence on individual freedom. Elsewhere he goes further, suggesting that all four varṇas are present 'in all men in different degrees of development' (Rādhākrishnan 1940: 366).

Conclusion

The reinterpretation of caste found in Vivekānanda and Rādhākrishnan, and in much Hindu writing in English today, replaces the concept of jāti with a concept of qualitative varṇa, while often continuing to use the term *caste*. Using a strategy typical of neo-Hinduism, it takes a feature of Hinduism which is already subject to attack from Western and Indian critics. It then shows that what the critics should attack is not the essence of that feature, but the inessentials and errors that have accumulated round it: in this case the multiplicity of jātis, most or all of the rules of purity, the disabilities of low jātis, the privileges of high jātis, and usually the hereditary principle. The objection to privilege can be met in one of two ways. One may say that privilege has no place in true caste, as Gāndhi does when he upholds hereditary membership of the varṇas and says that all should be equally valued (Iyer 1986: 22; 600-603), or one may say that privileges belong naturally to those who are spiritually or intellectually developed, as Vivekānanda does when he justifies the practice of giving to brahmins on the grounds that they are intellectual leaders (Vivekānanda, 'On charity': III, 305).

Reinterpretations of traditional concepts are not peculiar to the modern period.

> Gandhiji and Radhakrishnan are both in the Indian tradition when they use old words with new connotations and thus present themselves as true (i.e. orthodox) Hindus, although, in fact, they have risen far above the orthodoxy of traditional Hinduism (Wadia 1952: 777).

However, modern conditions provide fertile ground for the growth of such reinterpretations, and strong incentives for their production. They are a sign of the continuing adaptability and vitality of Hinduism. Reinterpretation involves the use of ancient texts, and also ancient and well-attested ideas: in this case, that varṇa is the origin of jāti, that varṇa depends not on birth but on quality, or even on individual preference, this last view being corroborated by the traditional etymology which connects *varṇa* with the root *vṛ* 'to choose'. The differences between varṇa and jāti are accounted for by the traditional idea that institutions which formerly reflected the sanātana dharma have become degenerate in the Kali age.

CHANGE AND CONTINUITY IN HINDU MARRIAGE RITUALS

Werner Menski

Introduction: Ritual innovation and resilience in British Asian laws

Lecturing on South Asian laws in London, I found more and more of my students interested in how South Asians in Britain interact with the English legal system and to what extent they preserve, develop or abandon the Hindu, Sikh and Muslim elements of their traditions. I have recently written in some detail about the legal side of this topic and have become quite critical of the way in which mainstream legal scholarship largely ignores the concerns of Asians in Britain (Menski 1988a, 1988b, 1991). Earlier, I had reported on some of my fieldwork among South Asians in Britain, focusing on legal pluralism in Hindu marriages (Menski 1987). Here, I present an outline of how traditional Hindu marriage rituals have developed over time and how they appear in Britain today, more or less loosely interlinked with the modern legal systems of India and England, as a vigorous arena of ritual change about which we know far too little. In other words, I am seeking to encourage more research in this field and would argue that it cannot be left entirely to social scientists who do not know Sanskrit and/or at least a modern South Asian language to do detailed fieldwork on this topic.

My argument is, in essence, that the observable ritual modifications of Hindu marriage rituals in Britain are only to a certain extent due to the new socio-legal environment of 'Inglistan', as some South Asians now call the country of the British, which has also become their own. Hindu marriages in Britain mainly differ from their South Asian prototypes because the official formal registration of marriages, confusingly also referred to as 'solemnization', is a compulsory element of the state law in England. Apart from this, it seems that the English law of marriage has hardly been able to disturb the customary patterns of Hindu marriage solemnization. In fact, English law, in a not uncharacteristic form of double standards, not wishing to admit diversity where the so-called 'common law' prevails, has officially denied legal validity to Hindu forms of marriage by requiring a formal secular act of registration of all marriages, while at the same time recognizing their importance.

This recognition was seen in 1972, when the English legal system explicitly accepted, through the Court of Appeal decision in *Kaur* v. *Singh* ([1972] *All ER* 292), that a marriage among Asians in Britain (in this case Sikhs) did not achieve full legal validity until there had been a customary, religious form of marriage solemnization as well as the legally required act of registration. In other words, the English state law has acknowledged the continuing potential of the performance of Hindu marriage rituals as an indicator of acquisition of the status of being married. As a result, English courts have had to decide a surprisingly large and growing number of cases in which Indian or 'Asian' law is involved, one of the most recent being reported in *The Times* (5 February 1991). Here a Sikh husband claimed that he had not validly married his wife in India twenty-five years previously, since they had only gone round the Guru Granth Sahib twice instead of four times, as is customary. The judge, in this case, was shown a photo album of the alleged wedding and spotted some flower petals on the dress of the groom, which led him to the conclusion that the marriage must have been completed, since the couple must have been blessed in the customary way, signifying the completion of the wedding ceremony and thus the legal validity of the marriage. Clearly, the topic of marriage solemnization among Asians in Britain has now gained new relevance in a quite unexpected way.

The qualified legal recognition accorded to Hindu forms of marriage solemnization in Britain seems to have become necessary, initially, because Hindus (as other 'Asians', and in fact all other 'ethnic minorities') have only gradually learnt to follow the secular English law on marriage registration. The Court of Appeal's decision in 1972 in *Kaur* (see above) could therefore be interpreted as expressing an expectation that Asians would eventually learn the new state law and abandon their traditions. But we now know that Asians have undergone this learning process without abandoning the customary forms of marriage solemnization (Menski 1988a) and that Britain is now a truly plural society (CRE 1990). In principle, Shirley Firth's work shows the same pattern for death rituals: awareness that one has to follow the 'law of the land' does not mean abandonment of one's customary traditions, whatever they may be, but a vigorous process of seeking to accommodate the needs of two legal and social systems.

Thus, as I have shown earlier (Menski 1987), Hindus in Britain have been under no official pressure to abandon their customary forms of marriage solemnization (as they were, apparently, in some parts of the Empire), but have been able to develop their rituals further, well outside the context of state control and (as I am arguing here) to such an extent that the 'inside view' of the matter today begins to be that the legal requirements of English law have been built into the Hindu marriage rituals. We have then, as I have recently shown elsewhere, nominal compliance with the English law, but in reality we can now witness the genesis, if not full development, of British Asian laws, with their own peculiar characteristics (Menski 1991).

I emphasized above that the changed legal environment is only one of the many factors contributing to ritual change. An equally powerful agent of ritual development is arguably the fact of living in diaspora and with it the at times distressing lack of guidance on matters of 'tradition'. As the work of Shirley Firth (p. 62) clearly shows, this can have haunting effects for individuals who do not know how to handle death rituals. Similarly, some evidence of ritual insecurity in the field of marriage solemnization does exist, but the implications are perhaps less frightening and there are many indications that such lacunae have been filled more easily by Hindu ritual experts in Britain, not only priests but old women. The field of Hindu marriage solemnization, then, offers a rich crop of evidence about ritual changes and modifications in the new socio-legal context in which British Asians find themselves. There are important implications here for the study of Sanskrit traditions in the modern world; it cannot be emphasized enough that much more work needs to be done in this field.

As a result of such ritual developments, Hindus in Britain today marry twice, as it were, and often appear to divorce twice too. But this perception (Menski 1987) may no longer be adequate today. It now seems as though Hindus in Britain are gradually and more consciously incorporating the legal requirements of the state law into their own modified forms of marriage solemnization. This is an important element of what I now call the new 'Asian laws in Britain' (Menski 1991). The most fascinating aspect of this for our present context is the fact that these modification processes are taking place within the ritual field and within the conceptual framework of sanskritic traditions and/or their customary equivalents.

All this may be quite contrary to what standard developmental models of rational progression would seem to suggest, but it is observable reality; rather than mono-directional westernizing and secularizing patterns, we can see here how traditional and modern elements together are used to recreate ritual patterns that conform to the notion of tradition. In other words, what we find is not 'pure' ritual continuity, despite a lot of rhetoric from some individuals who make such claims, but a modification of traditional patterns which is facilitated, in the Hindu case, by the traditional and age-old pattern of diversity and flexibility of customary forms of marriage solemnization.

While we want to focus on diversity and change in British Hindu marriage rituals, we must start here with an explicit recognition of the customary diversity in this field in traditional, mediaeval and modern India. To that extent, there is a fundamental continuity of tradition here which must be understood in its full implication: there was never such a thing as a 'standard' form of Hindu marriage. In other words, we cannot view traditional marriage rituals as a more or less static arena. Quite the opposite! As Shirley Firth shows for death rituals also (pp. 60, 64f), there has always been tremendous regional, local and status diversity, with a myriad modifications introduced by village, clan and even family customs, caste (in both senses; see Dermot Killingley's paper, p. 8), and a number of other considerations.

As a result, as we well know, no two Hindu marriage rituals are really exactly alike, a fact which creates its own problems in the study of this subject, if one talks about customs. In law, these are supposed to be forms of behaviour followed since time immemorial (in English law), or at least 'for a long time', as section 3 of the *HMA* (*Hindu Marriage Act* 1955) in India now stipulates more appropriately. The *HMA* also requires customs to have some degree of certainty and to be not against public policy. In reality, however, customs are much more flexible than most people imagine.

In Hindu law, due to the concept of dharma, it is customary that there cannot be any one binding model for all situations, least of all in the field of marriage, with its many nuances of status that are marked ritually and socially and may be overlooked far too easily (Derrett 1970: 296f).

We shall see, then, that classical Hindu law favoured continuous ritual innovation and flexibility and that the modern reforms of Hindu law in India in 1955-6 have shown considerable respect for these traditional patterns, though the motive was probably not so much respect for tradition itself as a realization on the part of the law-makers that they would be unable to introduce effective legal reforms in the central areas of marriage and divorce law overnight, if at all. Since there was no change in the law, there was then, perhaps, also no need to modify marriage rituals as a result of a new legal environment. This does not mean to say that there have been no recent changes in marriage rituals in India, but the nature of the changes in India may be different from those in Britain, where Asians have apparently found ways to 'sanskritize' the originally secular rituals of the Registry Office.

Hindu marriage solemnization in India

We have remarkably well-documented material about the traditional Hindu law of marriage from Vedic times onwards and there is a huge literature on Hindu marriage. Already, the ancient Vedic literature contains two ideal models of marriage solemnization in *ṚV* 10, 85 and *AV* 14. I have retranslated and analysed those texts in the first volume of my PhD thesis (Menski 1984, esp. pp. 218-394) and have shown there how, very subtly, the brahmin priests gradually gained control of the solemnization of Hindu marriages. From a starting point, *after* the consummation of the marriage, as ritual scapegoats for the removal of magical defilements and dangers connected with the bridal, virginal blood, they gradually moved to the position we know today, where even *before* the marriage, they take on a protecting role. In other words, the original emphasis on a de-polluting role has been shed in favour of an altogether more auspicious involvement that sets in as early as possible.

These ancient Vedic texts also tell us much about the origins of particular rites of marriage that we find performed even today. I found that some rituals that are considered important today were probably not yet developed in the Vedic models. For example, the famous ritual of the seven steps (saptapadī) is certainly absent in *ṚV* 10, 85; an early form of it may be seen in the *AV* text. It is only fully developed, quite clearly, in the next layer of Sanskrit literature that focuses on this topic.

Several centuries later, the important handbooks on domestic rites (gṛhyasūtras) and some related texts contain modified models of marriage solemnization and present them in a different style. While the Vedic texts were basically just the mantras that may have been spoken, and we are not told about the ritual actions accompanying them, now we find more detailed indications of ritual actions, while a knowledge of the relevant Vedic mantras is to a large extent presupposed. Such mantras are then quoted in short form when they come from the same Vedic school as the sūtra text. This is why indologists speak of Ṛgvedic or Yajurvedic gṛhyasūtras; but this distinction breaks down somewhat because all gṛhyasūtras use most of the mantras of *ṚV* 10, 85 and many others from *AV* 14.

Since there are also quite a few new mantras in these texts, we must imagine the development of the sanskritic tradition in rather fragmentary form, i.e., that selected elements of the mantra material as well as of ritual actions have been reassembled over time into slightly different rituals. Since this was, and continues to be, a very complex ongoing process, the ritual diversity within Hindu marriage solemnization patterns would inevitably increase to a point where it became virtually impossible to determine with any degree of certainty what belonged to which ritual school and which textual tradition. For even today, if one were to take any of the ritual sūtras as a basis on which to reconstruct a 'traditional' ritual (as some Hindu priests have been doing), one would be lost for guidance on the side of ritual actions and would need to harmonize the somewhat sterile sanskritic ritual model with the needs of the particular community and/or couple. As a result, most Hindu priests today, as far as I can see, use a variety of textual sources and models to construct an appropriate Hindu marriage ritual for the particular occasion.

No one gṛhyasūtra provides exactly the same model for marriage solemnization as another sūtra, and several texts indicate that there are other ritual traditions that may be followed on points of detail. Since there is a large number of such specialist texts, the question naturally arises of how authoritative any one text may be. If we compare the ritual details of marriage solemnization, we find a fairly general pattern that is repeated, albeit with many modifications, almost everywhere. In other words, sanskritic models of marriage solemnization in classical India reached a stage of ritual elaboration on similar lines to one another; individual texts contain a large number of variations of a generally accepted common framework or basic structure. Clearly, in matters of ritual detail, 'the greatest divergence prevailed from very ancient times' (Kane 1941: 527). There has never been much scope for seeking to create one uniform marriage ritual for all Hindus; in fact, there is evidence to the contrary, because some texts stress, for example, that different varṇas should solemnize marriages in different ways.

In the secondary literature, several authors have sought to tell us what this basic structure contains, but unfortunately, the various attempts at listing all possible marriage rituals together (e.g., Kane 1941: 531-8 and Pandey 1969: 207-25) have produced interesting but quite confusing conglomerates that do not reflect real life in any way. It must again be emphasized that because of the influence of local and other customary practices, no two Hindu marriage rituals will be exactly alike. There is fluidity and flexibility in the minutiae of the customary patterns. On the other hand, we do find that some elements of ritual have a prominent place in the literature. The major elements appear to be:

kanyādāna	the giving away of the girl;
pāṇigrahaṇa	holding the bride's hand;
lājāhoma	sacrifice to the fire god Agni as a celestial witness;
agnipariṇayana	the clockwise circumambulation of the fire;

saptapadī the taking of the seven steps.

Listing these five major ritual elements here creates its own problems, however. What if any one of the above was not performed? Would we still have a 'proper' and legally valid Hindu marriage? The answer to this must definitely be in the affirmative. Firstly, all these rituals appear in variant forms (on the saptapadī modifications, see in detail Menski 1984: 580-624). Secondly, while an ideal, high-caste Hindu marriage ritual would contain all these rituals in one form or another, there are many Hindu marriage rituals in which some of the above elements, or even all of them, are missing. These would still be Hindu marriages. Thus, distinctions between ceremonious and simpler Hindu marriages can be made, and they are relevant and meaningful in their specific socio-ritual Hindu context. As outsiders, we cannot ignore the fact that very many Hindu marriages are not elaborately ceremonialized. Further, we must be careful not to see this as an aberrant deviation from the norm, but should recognize it as part of the normative diversity of Hindu ritual traditions.

While the realization of this diversity is nothing new, and everyone pays lip-service to the importance of traditional Hindu ritual diversity, unfortunately much of the secondary literature on Hindu marriage has given undue emphasis to the elitist perception that all Hindu marriages must be full-fledged sanskritic ritual dramas. In principle, this particular perception is comparable to that of historians who have traditionally studied elite phenomena, such as kings and queens and other important figures in history, and are now turning to the common man's concerns and role in history. The study of the living traditions of Hindu marriage rituals as performed by common Hindus is still in its infancy and should constitute an exciting new field of study, both in India and in the Hindu diaspora.

The Vedic texts on marriage solemnization are silent on how authoritative or binding they were or may have been in real life. The texts are mantra collections, with hardly any implied commentary, though *AV* 14 does contain some hints in this regard. It appears that we must see the Vedic ritual models as ideal models; it cannot be assumed that all Hindus at any time solemnized their marriages in accordance with those texts.

This ideal model nature of the texts is continued by the gṛhyasūtras, but we now find some explicit statements about the relationship of the sanskritic textual models and real marriages. Thus *AGS* 1, 7, 1-2 states:

> Now, manifold indeed are the customs of different areas and villages; those one should observe at the marriage. Only what is common, that we shall state here.

This statement, and similar indications elsewhere, tell us that local, regional and caste variations have abounded all the time and that there has never been a uniform pattern of Hindu marriage solemnization. However, such indications in the texts of their own limits as models are, in my view, extremely important evidence for our understanding of the role of such ancient Indian texts. What does it mean that a text only states what is 'common'? The Sanskrit term used here (*samāna*) could be interpreted in a number of ways, but certainly does not mean, in my view, that the gṛhyasūtra texts impose universally binding rules for the solemnization of Hindu marriages.

The various layers of texts following the sūtras in time and substance have not been as helpful as one might expect in throwing light on the above questions. The vast śāstric literature, in particular, contains only a few general comments on marriage solemnization here and there. Contrary to general belief, the dharmaśāstras do not concern themselves with the rituals of marriage solemnization; that was the business of the gṛhyasūtras and the specialized literature that follows them, i.e., the various texts called *vivāha-paddhati* (of which there are hundreds, it appears), *vivāha-prayoga* or *gṛhya-prayoga*.

One of the rare explicit statements on Hindu marriage in the dharmaśāstras is found in *Manu* 8, 227. Here, in the context of contractual relations, it is said that

> The nuptial texts are a certain proof (that a maiden has been made a lawful) wife; but the learned should know that they (and the marriage-ceremony) are complete with the seventh step (of the bride around the sacred fire).

Unfortunately, this translation, taken from a standard work (Bühler 1886: 295), is quite misleading in a number of ways. We shall return to this below. The impression created here is, no doubt, that all Hindu marriages contain, and culminate in, a saptapadī.

Other texts that seem relevant explore some minor ritual detail and often debate minutiae of priestly expertise. By focusing on such details, the view of the whole ceremony is lost. No ancient text, as far as I know, discusses marriage solemnization theoretically. But there are some texts of mediaeval origin that contemplate certain theoretical aspects. Thus Gadādhara, a seventeenth-century Bengali writer, discusses the sacramental nature of marriage (saṃskāra) and provides a new and interesting emphasis on the more philosophical and psychological explanations of what happens during a Hindu marriage ritual (Derrett 1976). In a way, such rationalizations also provide, it seems, new justifications for the elaborate performance of such rituals.

Persistent elite perceptions that Hindu marriage is a sacrament and that all Hindu marriages are complex ritual dramas have been carried into our time. These impressions are strengthened by currently used handbooks or manuals; these may be either faithful copies of a particular gṛhyasūtra, or modified elaborate ritual models, possibly even in a regional language rather than Sanskrit (for two examples, see Menski 1984: 849-79).

Naturally, we would not expect such handbooks to discuss their own irrelevance to many Hindus, though we saw above that there may be such indications already in the gṛhyasūtras. It is also natural that non-sanskritic rituals, orally transmitted, are not well-documented. So we have to look outside the Sanskrit literature for guidance on the use of elaborate ritual models. Unfortunately, not much fieldwork has been done on this, though we seem to have an unexplored plethora of material in the many District Gazetteers and other handbooks of district administrators that contain immensely valuable indications of the living traditions of Hindu marriage and their community-wise differentiations. The legal literature, more precisely the Anglo-Indian case-law and modern Indian law books, has had to grapple with this problem in a way that reflects social reality much more accurately than the sanskritic literature.

Of course, this is not the right place to go into the problem in detail. But let us note that doubts about the legal validity of a particular marriage might arise where a full sanskritic marriage ritual had not been performed, for whatever reason. Deliberate omission of a crucial ritual might make a marriage ceremony a mere sham, or it might signify a different status for that union, as I have already pointed out at the beginning of this paper with reference to the recent Sikh case. Inadvertent oversight might render the ritual ineffective, or have no effect whatsoever. The Hindu public, 'who never allowed the shastric view of marriage to occupy the whole field' (Derrett 1970: 349), subtly distinguished between different kinds of Hindu marriages (Derrett 1970: 297). Thus, the more we look, the more evidence of the diversity of Hindu traditions we will find.

Under British rule, Anglo-Indian courts gradually built up a body of case-law in which this matter was discussed, not directly, but mainly as a preliminary issue in cases about money and status. Was a particular child a legitimate heir? Was the woman before the court a legally wedded wife, or merely a concubine? Frequently, huge sums of money and much power were at stake, as historical research by Pamela Price (1979) and other scholars has shown. The weaker party, frequently the woman, often lost good cases. A male-oriented, sanskritic approach was taken by the courts, so that judicial opinion favoured the performers of full-fledged sanskritic rituals despite evidence that many customary rituals did not contain such sanskritic elements. The issue was never quite resolved during the British raj.

An issue which we also cannot discuss in detail here is the relationship of sanskritic and customary rituals, and the Indian courts' view of this relationship. Many sanskritic rituals became customary, or became at least an integral part of customary traditions; sanskritization must have played a role here too. Yet many customary traditions remained marginally sanskritic, totally unaffected by scriptural models, or even developed in reaction to such models, as recent evidence from Madras (the self-respecters' movement; see Mangalamurugesan 1980) and other parts of India shows (for the neo-Buddhists of Maharashtra, see the interesting case of *Baby* v. *Jayant* in *AIR* 1985 Bombay 283). Further, in certain situations it may have been customary to have minimal rituals (see Derrett 1970: 297), or even no rituals at all. This would be the case, inter alia, where either spouse had been widowed or divorced. There are clear indications that in such cases mere cohabitation may be the expected norm; in other words, there may be a 'zero-ritual' as the customary form of Hindu marriage solemnization (see Menski 1983).

The British sought to respect the customary Hindu law of marriage and did not interfere in solemnization patterns. Yet their restrictive approach to the recognition of custom has been causing problems almost up to the present day. As late as 1969, the Calcutta High Court held that custom, to be legally recognized, had to be followed from ancient times, and had to be obligatory in a certain caste, community or sub-caste (Diwan 1982: 81). This approach completely overlooks the fluidity and diversity of Hindu customary practices and has only recently, it appears, been abandoned by the Indian Supreme Court in the case of *Sumitra Devi* (*AIR* 1985 Supreme Court 765).

The modern Hindu law in India was codified to a large extent in 1955-6. However, as I have shown above (p. 34), it is significant that Hindu marriage solemnization in India has entirely been left to custom. This shows awareness of the strength of customary rules, and of their diversity. It amounts to an official admission of inability to regulate the most central aspect of family law uniformly for all Hindus. Thus the validity of Hindu marriages in India depends, as before, on the question of whether a customary marriage ritual has been performed or not.

The relevant enactment is section 7 of the *HMA*:

> 7. Ceremonies for a Hindu marriage.
> (1) A Hindu marriage may be solemnized in accordance with the customary rites and ceremonies of either party thereto.
> (2) Where such rites and ceremonies include the *saptapadi* (that is, the taking of seven steps by the bridegroom and the bride jointly before the sacred fire), the marriage becomes complete and binding when the seventh step is taken.

The first sub-section says clearly enough that the performance of the customary rituals of either party shall be considered to create a valid union. This leaves the parties (should a case go to court, which is by no means normal) to prove the customary nature of what was performed. The onus here, ultimately, is on the Indian judiciary to ascertain the customs of particular castes, or even families. This is a huge task, and one for which modern Indian judges are not well equipped. As a result, we have had a large number of unsatisfactory decisions, even of the Supreme Court. The two leading cases on this matter, *Bhaurao Shankar* (*AIR* 1965 Supreme Court 1564) and *Kanwal Ram* (*AIR* 1966 Supreme Court 614), now stand with questionable authority since *Sumitra Devi*'s case of 1985 (see three paragraphs above), which did not explicitly overrule the two leading cases, but seems to me to have that effect. Not surprisingly, the major problems are whether customary rituals can be changed or updated, and to what extent they have to follow the sanskritic models which section 7 (2) of the *HMA* mistakenly stipulates. In either case, the issue is how flexible Hindu ritual tradition or custom may be.

In the Indian cases that discussed this problem to some extent, the situation was always that a husband had married his second wife in a ritually defective ceremony, raising the question whether that marriage was valid in law. If it was, the husband would be guilty of bigamy and should go to jail. In *Bhaurao Shankar* (see previous paragraph), the question was whether neo-Buddhist marriage ceremonies that had evolved during the past five to ten years could be seen as customary. In 1965, the court did not wish to recognize these 'new' customs as legally valid; thus it let the bigamous husband off the hook. In *Kanwal Ram* (see previous paragraph), it was held that even where it had been admitted by the husband that he had entered into a bigamous marriage, such a marriage was not capable of being valid in law, since some technical detail of marriage solemnization was missing. Such formal legalistic approaches were very questionable and must of necessity serve as evidence that a male-oriented judiciary, concerned to avoid jail sentences for Hindu bigamists, cared little about the women involved in such marriages.

However, in the case of *Baby* (p. 39 above) in 1981, the Bombay High Court had before it another bigamy prosecution arising from the same neo-Buddhist community as in *Bhaurao Shankar*. This time it was found that the 'new' marriage rituals of the former low-caste Hindus had to be accepted as customary rites and ceremonies under modern Hindu law. Thus, it was held that the offence of bigamy had been committed where the 'new' Buddhist custom of marriage solemnization had been followed twice. The court was impressed by detailed evidence of the marriage rituals, by the realization that such rituals had now been observed for more than twenty-five years, and by the fact that they had been followed by a large community. Not to hold such marriages valid would have bastardized a large number of children and would have caused much harm to women. So this High Court case represented a more liberal and more compassionate view than the earlier Supreme Court cases. Finally, in 1985, the Indian Supreme Court indicated in the case of *Sumitra Devi* (p. 40 above, at p. 766 of the judgment) that it had now understood the ritual diversity of Hindu marriage solemnization better and held that

> There is no doubt that in order that there may be a valid marriage according to Hindu law, certain religious rites have to be performed. Invoking the fire and performing Saptapadi around the sacred fire have been considered by this Court to be two of the basic requirements for a traditional marriage. It is equally true that there can be a marriage acceptable in law according to customs which do not insist on performance of such rites as referred to above and marriages of this type give rise to legal relations which law accepts.

As I have said before, Indian judges would not necessarily be well qualified to consider details of ritual and ceremony in Hindu marriages. Since even family customs are recognizable as valid law, how on earth is one going to ascertain, given the fluid nature of customs, and the customary element of ad hoc improvization when it comes to some details, that a particular marriage solemnization has *strictly* followed established custom in every detail? No clear answers have been given on this point, but the court's decision in *Sumitra Devi* gives rise to some hope. My own view is that in cases of minor modification one must not take a legalistic, technical approach. Does not watching Hindu marriage rituals, whether in India or in Britain, create an impression that there is a degree of haphazardness that is part of the ritual process? It may not be a good idea to look rigidly at individual rites within a complex ritual sequence; rather, it seems preferable to consider whether the totality of the marriage rituals performed in any given case would create, in the eyes of the community or family concerned, a valid marital union. This, happily, is what even British judges have learnt today when faced with questions of the validity of Hindu marriages.

One of the best indicators of legal validity must surely be that cohabitation between the spouses has taken place after solemnization of the marriage. This is, apparently, as true in Britain today as in India; in both cases concern about female chastity is of central importance. But the fact of consummation of the marriage itself has not been accepted by Indian courts as an indicator of legal validity of a union. Nor would it be a convincing argument in an English court.

Under section 7 (2) of the *HMA* (see p. 40), special problems have arisen over the nature of the Hindu ritual of saptapadī. The wording of the section clearly indicates that the saptapadī need not be a part of all customary Hindu marriages. As we saw earlier, leading cases were mistaken and have held otherwise; one wonders why the section has been included at all. Marriage rituals are normally complete when the rituals have all been performed, but in the Hindu case this is difficult to ascertain. As there are quite a few pre-nuptial rites, so we also find many post-nuptial rituals and ceremonies. Are they part of marriage solemnization or not? The law-makers in 1955 clearly looked to *Manu* 8, 227 (p. 38 above) for guidance and made their complex task easy by simply incorporating the opinion stated in that text into the modern law. The śāstric statement, however, does little else than pinpoint one ritual element which shall signify the fact of legally binding marriage; i.e., it seeks to determine from which point in the ritual onwards the contract of marriage will be legally binding. In all those cases where the saptapadī is not a customary element, we have thus got to find another means of ascertaining when a marriage should be seen as legally valid and completed. I have said above that the completion of the rituals per se appears to be sufficient indication for this purpose.

But then, what actually is meant by the 'seventh step'? This is a very difficult issue. I do not have the space here to explain this in detail, but this much may be said. Today, the single Sanskrit term *saptapadī* refers to a variety of ritual models. I have evidence that rituals of that name have, over time, taken a variety of forms. What, for example, did the Indian Supreme Court in *Sumitra Devi* (p. 41 above) mean by performing saptapadī 'around the sacred fire'? This seems different from what section 7 (2) of *HMA* stipulated, namely, taking seven steps 'before the sacred fire'. If the traditional saptapadī in its original form is carried out in linear fashion, away from the fire, how is it possible that we are given an impression today of a ritual taking place 'around' the fire? Here again, ritual variations over time have developed: in many communities the circumambulations of the fire (the traditional agni-pariṇayana) and the ritual of the seven steps (the traditional saptapadī) have become amalgamated into seven circumambulations of the fire, which are now also called saptapadī. I have even come to know of attempts to introduce another variant: a priest suggested trying to achieve the circumambulation of the holy fire in seven steps! Here again is further proof of the constant development of sanskritic traditions and of the scope for 'specialist' interference with traditional models. Of course, the single circumambulation of the fire in seven steps has not found much favour. This kind of modification probably went too far and created its own problems: what, then, do you do about the four rounds, often called *pherās*, that most couples make round the fire?

Generally speaking, the interpretation of section 7 of the *HMA* by the Indian courts shows a presumption in favour of elaborate sanskritic marriage rituals—possibly a result of the elite status of members of the judiciary themselves. There was initially no admission by the courts that marriage rituals may not be uniformly observed and followed. When the case-law created obvious problems, we found, firstly, that section 7 became amended for Tamil Nadu in 1967 by the *Hindu Marriage (Madras Amendment) Act*, which inserted section 7A, making explicit allowance for simple, non-sanskritic forms of marriage solemnization in that state. Secondly, as I showed above, the Indian case-law itself has now been modified to account for the ritual diversity and fluidity in Hindu marriage solemnization.

Clearly, many forms of simple and non-sanskritic marriage solemnization continue to exist in India and are apparent in Britain. My own, fairly limited, fieldwork on this in Gujarat, Maharashtra, Kerala and Britain has yielded much evidence of locally divergent and caste-specific patterns. But this is not a topic that lawyers tend to be excited about and a detailed study of sanskritic ritual changes clearly demands the attention of a sanskritist.

To the extent that we shift emphasis to the study of low-status groups of Hindus, we are also likely to obtain more evidence of simple Hindu marriage rituals in which the sanskritic elements may be partly or totally absent. But there is also increasing evidence of a trend for ritual elaboration in such communities. A major reason for this is apparently that Hindu marriage is not only a religious ritual, but also a public event of great importance. First of all, it serves to 'register' the marriage in the eyes of the community, which is all that counts in the Hindu context. Secondly, marriages are social events of great significance and importance for all participants. A marriage is a splendid occasion for affirming or asserting one's claim to standing in society, enabling people to display status in so many ways, and consequently there is much evidence of increase in ritual and ceremonial spectacle (tamāśā). Marriage solemnization here becomes an aspect of 'conspicuous consumption', with the result that sanskritic ritual elements may be introduced into traditional, local customary rituals as a status indicator rather than proof of greater traditionality. In tandem with this, new and quite costly 'secular' customs have been developing, such as sending expensive invitation cards for weddings rather than the customary personal visit for that purpose.

On the other hand, there are indications of processes of modernization leading to simpler forms of marriage. The Tamil self-respecters represent a good example here. The Ārya Samāj wedding is being advocated, both in India and in the UK, as a 'simple' and less ritualistic (but nevertheless 'pure' and possibly just as costly) modification of established customary traditions (Cormack 1961: 123).

The flexibility of arrangements may be illustrated by the case of a brahmin couple from Gujarat. The husband had been widowed; the wife was about forty years old, had not been previously married and was a virgin. Out of respect for his deceased wife, the husband preferred not to have an elaborate Hindu wedding. So the couple registered their marriage under the secular *Special Marriage Act* of 1954. This had the obvious effect of creating legal validity of the union without any Hindu form of marriage solemnization. But the wife would have felt bad about performing no rites at all, so the couple arranged to have what might be called today a 'church blessing', a little ad hoc ceremony of short duration, to which some friends and relatives were invited. Only a few rituals were performed, by no means a complete ceremony, but the wife clearly felt that this kind of truncated ceremony was appropriate in the circumstances. Had she been a widow or divorcée herself, there would have been fewer or indeed no rituals. Since she was a virgin bride, she felt the need to have a 'sanskritic' wedding—in her words, a Hindu vivāha. It made no difference to her that the marriage had been registered before; she felt married only after the religious ceremony. The same appears to be true for Hindu couples in Britain today who are undergoing two types of marriage solemnization. In either case, the detail of the sanskritic ceremony seems to matter less than the fact that one does 'something'.

To summarize this section, then, we can say that the traditional Hindu law of marriage solemnization continues in full force, but with many modifications, in modern India today. Far from being a uniform, static tradition, this is a complex conglomerate of sanskritic and local/caste customary practices that show quite considerable flexibility, in view of the particular circumstances of the spouses and their families, with virtually no interference from the state law. Thus, a wide variety of modes of marriage solemnization can lead to a valid Hindu marriage. We might see them on a sliding scale between the extremes of splendidly elaborated sanskritic wedding and simple ritualization of the fact that two people have now become husband and wife. In certain situations, as I have shown, there are obvious ritualistic reasons why elaborate rituals are not performed; in others, incomplete rituals may be purposely performed to signify an inferior status of the union. The resulting confusing diversity has caused problems for some Hindu spouses, generally women, who in subsequent struggles over property or status, were unable to establish their claim as legally married partners. This, too, is a relevant issue for British Asians today and shows how important a proper understanding of Hindu rituals has remained in the modern world.

Hindu marriage rituals in Britain

It is well known that Asians in Britain have mainly come from certain parts of the subcontinent, sometimes via another country, and that most of the Hindus in the UK originate from certain parts of Gujarat and Panjab. There are much smaller groups from Maharashtra, Bengal, Tamil Nadu, Uttar Pradesh and other places (Kanitkar and Jackson 1982). This means that we will find *certain* local customary practices from the subcontinent transplanted into the UK, not the whole range of practices of a local nature.

As in other migration processes of the kind Asians in Britain have been primarily involved in (the latest example of this appears to be Asian labour migration into Japan), it is apparent that the Indians who went abroad in search of 'greener pastures' were generally not the very poorest and most 'backward', but mainly members of the middle classes from a certain range of castes. Where indentured labour was originally involved, the pattern may well be different (Clarke, Peach and Vertovec (eds.) 1990), but the majority of Hindus in Britain have either come directly from India or via East Africa and are not from the lowest classes. As a result, we do not find, as we would in India, many low-caste and tribal people among our Hindu population in the UK. Such low-caste people as there are often have a middle-class background and are not generally from the poorest sections of their communities.

The implications of this for a study of Hindu marriage rituals in Britain are quite apparent: we just cannot find here many respondents, nor whole communities, that would exclusively follow local customary, non-sanskritic rituals. As a result, researchers are likely to find more evidence of sanskritic ritualization than may be the case in India.

Further, the element of conspicuous consumption in public or community celebrations means that in the UK, as in India, we will witness elaboration rather than simplification of marriage rituals. However, it remains to be seen, if we want to make this distinction, whether the more narrowly 'religious' rituals in this context are changing in the direction of secularization or whether we really find 'religious' ritual elaboration.

Of crucial importance to our study is the influence of English law on the matter. Clearly, Hindu customary rituals, however elaborate and sanskritized, have no legal validity in English law if performed in England and not accompanied by the secular registration ceremony. The concept of sacramental marriage is not unknown in England, but no English court would be prepared, one must assume, to uphold the validity of a Hindu marriage entered into in England simply on the basis that a Hindu marriage is a saṃskāra.

While English marriage law requires the registration of marriages, in a kind of avoidance reaction, large numbers of English people have started to cohabit rather than entering into legal marriages. This clearly defeats the administrative rationale of the state's marriage registration system and has caused many legal problems with which we are not concerned here. Hindus, however, could not follow this model of avoiding the state law, for two reasons. Firstly, they tend to be very concerned about female chastity; extra-marital sex by females would be quite unacceptable socially, a fact which causes many problems to Asian girls growing up in Britain. Secondly, in a modern welfare state so many rights of an individual depend on one's legal status, and many immigrants would have to pay dearly (as some now find) should there be any legal insecurity. As a result, we find conscious attempts by Asians to follow the law of the land as closely as possible.

Another very powerful factor has helped this learning process. In the 1960s and 1970s, some Hindus found to their dismay that their daughter or sister could simply be abandoned by her husband if the marriage had not been registered according to English law. It seems that there have been just a few early cases of this kind, none officially reported; they sent shockwaves through the communities, since it was soon found that the women and their families had no remedies under English law. The considerable element of shame involved in such instances has rapidly led to adaptation processes among Hindus in Britain.

The message, then, that the public official registration of a marriage is absolutely necessary, has successfully been transmitted by the official system, albeit in an odd way, i.e., because not to do so would invite many troubles. As an obvious result, most Asian marriages in Britain are now first registered, then solemnized in a religious ceremony.

The sequence itself is significant and meaningful in the context of traditional South Asian cultures. English law requires only a simple, secular ceremony of registration of the marriage. This is sometimes referred to as 'solemnization', but this is perhaps a euphemism. At any rate, the solemn and formal ceremony in the Registrar's chambers, at the end of which the groom may be formally encouraged to kiss the bride, must of necessity remain alien to most Hindus. But its crucial element is that it establishes the legal factum of the marital contract between the spouses on the one hand, and the state on the other. However, one cannot be so sure whether a marital contract between the spouses actually exists from the moment of registration in the minds of those spouses and their families. As I have described elsewhere (Menski 1987), after the ceremony of registration most Hindu spouses return to their respective homes; this seems to indicate that from the Hindu perspective the state's ceremony is rather like an engagement.

It is not surprising, then, that originally many families did not assign much importance to the registration ceremony. I have come across cases where people virtually got married during a lunch break, both parties going their own way immediately after they had been 'joined in matrimony'. Apparently, the registered wedding meant very little then; it remained a sort of necessary evil. More importantly, the spouses (as they are according to English law) do not see each other as husband and wife, and are not so seen by other Asians (Pearl 1986: 19; Menski 1987: 194). The nuptial contract between the spouses and their respective families is only concluded at the religious wedding

(Menski 1987: 195); in such cases there is no consummation of the marriage prior to the religious solemnization. This shows that Hindu customary traditions have quite successfully withstood the pressures of official English law, which, as all official laws do, claims supremacy and sees itself as paramount.

The fact that the legally existing marriage is somewhat held in abeyance by the requirement to have a religious wedding has caused a new problem in English law, which is of peripheral interest here. Clearly, such marriages now remain voidable in law and can still be called off by the families. Because of the time-lag between the registered marriage and the religious wedding, there is plenty of scope for things to go wrong. As a result, there have been hundreds of nullity petitions from Asians, attempts to undo the legally binding effects of the registration of such marriages. Often this has been because the families have fallen out for some reason, not that the spouses were dissatisfied with each other.

Clearly, this is an unsatisfactory situation on all counts. While English law has not clarified the issue after the 1972 *Kaur* case (p. 32), it appears that Hindu custom in Britain has developed in such a way as to take account of the potential problem. To avoid the dangers of the liminal phase between registration and religious solemnization, Hindus in Britain are currently learning that it is better to leave as little time as possible between official registration and religious ceremony. An ideal situation would obviously be to marry in a 'registered building', where registration and religious ceremony can be organized together, but it appears that many obstacles continue to be placed in the way of Hindus wishing to obtain that status for temples or community centres (Menski 1987: 191-3). There is a trend now to have the registered wedding on a Friday and the religious wedding during the immediately following weekend. In this way the liminal phase is significantly reduced, although there are no uniform patterns here and it is still not unusual to find a gap of several months between registration and solemnization.

This trend to bring the registration ceremony and the Hindu wedding as closely together as possible has apparently allowed an interesting new ritual development among Hindus in Britain. When a registration is closely followed by a religious ceremony, it becomes possible for the families involved to treat both ceremonies as one. We know that traditional Hindu weddings consist of many different rites that extend over days. A few more rituals added at some point need not make a significant difference to the whole ritual. In other words, it has been very simple to incorporate the English registration ceremony ritually into the rather more complex system of Hindu marriage solemnization. We shall look at this in more detail below (p. 50).

Both in India and in Britain, Hindus spend much time, effort and money in the manifold preparations for a wedding. The relationships between the wife-giving and the wife-receiving families are built in much the same way here as in India. The ritualization of a pre-nuptial stage also appears to continue in Britain, though I would like to see more fieldwork on this. There is now quite often considerable insecurity over what is the right thing to do, and long discussions and complex enquiries may be necessary. Advice is often sought from India in such situations, from old ladies in particular, who seem to act as custodians of tradition, a position acknowledged in the śāstric literature and in reality, as we saw above (p. 33).

When it comes to the wedding itself, we find first of all that it tends to be at a weekend, for several reasons of convenience. This now happens in India as well as in Britain. Since astrological advice is very often sought about auspicious days and times, the choice of suitable dates has become quite restricted, and there is a rush to book marriage halls and other facilities. Some Hindus override the astrological objections and marry 'out of season' and on inauspicious days; this regularly necessitates special propitiatory rituals. Some Hindu priests have declared themselves distinctly unhappy with this and several of them would do the necessary extra rituals as a means of ensuring, for themselves, that the risk remains entirely that of the spouses.

Generally speaking, the trend appears to be towards shorter marriage rituals, because of the much enlarged expense if they were to go on for a very long time. Again, similar developments are observable in India; it would require detailed comparative analysis to see if particular communities or families were developing a distinctly different marriage ritual in Britain. Since there is, in most communities, quite intensive interaction with Indian relatives and caste-fellows, we see much exchange of relevant ritual information, so that the impression I have is one of a parallel development between Indian and British traditions.

I find the role of the Hindu priests or pandits in this context undervalued. Hindu traditions, pervasive as they may be, do not maintain themselves automatically; they have to be maintained. In tandem with the old ladies, and older family members generally, the Hindu priests who solemnize marriages in Britain have become guardians of tradition in a very central sense. This tradition, in all its flexibility, is in a constant process of minor modification. So the pandit does not just sit there expounding scripture; rather he guides, almost imperceptibly, so that the crucial adjustment processes that have to take place in a new environment cause minimal imbalance and tension. For example, certain ritual ingredients that are freely available in India have been replaced by others in British rituals. A particular kind of grass or flower, unavailable in Britain, would be replaced by similar ingredients rather than being omitted altogether. So we find a number of subtly progressing adjustments in the ritual sphere. Typically for anything Hindu, there is no central regulation here, so the priests are helping to build modified traditions that may or may not stand the test of time and may become peculiar to their own clientèle. Much detailed fieldwork could be done in this area of inquiry.

When it comes to ritual actions during the performance of the marriage rituals, some priests have been instrumental in introducing a particular sequence of rituals, or even a particular ritual not used before, or in omitting a particular rite. If the families concerned accept this, and the old ladies as vigilant guardians of family and

elements taken out astrological advice, long rituals

adjustment to material for weddings rituals

adaptions by priests

caste customs are satisfied, we may in effect find a new tradition that is to a large extent priest-made. Generally speaking, though, this is a coordinated effort by priest and family members together; a priest who wanted to introduce a really new element, as Shirley Firth shows (p. 77), might run into difficulties.

Hindu priests who solemnize marriages in different communities, as probably most of them do, tend to emphasize differential ritual structures for different client groups. It is not the case that a particular Hindu priest will perform a standard ritual for all the communities he serves. An experienced priest will adjust to the particular family or community and will perpetuate the many subtle customary modifications that signify the varṇa or jāti status of the participants and their local origins. Again, these are processes provided for in the sūtra literature, and there is nothing new here in the British Hindu experience.

My impression is that rather than following a rigid customary model of sanskritic-cum-local customary rituals, the priest, the spouses and their families will negotiate ad hoc a suitable and therefore appropriate (from the point of view of dharma) marriage ceremony. Certain doubts as to its customary nature may then, indeed, be justified, but I am not troubled by that. By now it should have become clear that Hindu customary law is inherently diverse and so flexible that it may appear as a haphazard ad hoc arrangement rather than what we in the West expect of 'custom' by way of certainty and rigidity.

The negotiated end-result is likely to contain all or most of the major sanskritic rituals that I listed above, but this is by no means always the case in Britain. Even the ritual that has been officially considered so crucial and important, the saptapadī, is either not performed at all in many cases, or in a form that was not contemplated by the gṛhyasūtras.

The fact that Hindu marriage rituals are performed in public not only signifies community recognition of the marriage (which I would call 'indigenous registration'), but also ensures a large extent of cultural continuity. While manifestly unfamiliar rituals may be rejected on the spot, some new ostentatious ritual variants have emerged in Britain as a result of preoccupation with status rather than religious standing. The abolition of the pound note created some problems in this context. Not only had it become customary to give such notes as presents to maintain traditional patterns of gift exchange; one also garlanded the groom with them. As a result the Scottish pound note, still in circulation, has become an extremely desirable currency! Another example would be the ritualization of the ubiquitous reception, in which the circumambulation of the wedding cake (clearly a British innovation) might now be a feature, though I have only seen it performed once. There is quite unlimited scope here for the development of manifestly untraditional traditions, though again we must remember that the same processes have been going on in India.

There is not much evidence of Hindu marriage rituals being abandoned altogether in Britain. A few cases of couples having only a registered wedding cannot be seen as evidence of ritual decline in the community, especially if we remind ourselves of the many Indian cases in which rituals are not considered appropriate.

I have asked pandits how they use Sanskrit texts in the course of marriage solemnization. Here again, we find remarkable flexibility. A priest will not normally rely on any one particular text from beginning to end, even though it is a specialized manual for weddings. Quite evidently, most pandits have developed their own combination of mantras from a variety of sources in a remarkably eclectic fashion. Here also, tradition is being updated; there is much scope for an interesting comparative study here. While most priests have been trained in India, we have some very active 'self-made' pandits and a growing number of trainee pandits in Britain.

Much energy is now spent on explaining to the spouses and guests (if they care to listen) what particular mantras 'mean', or why one performs particular rituals. I am not convinced that people get a fair deal here, as the ubiquitous information that a particular ritual is performed for 'good luck and prosperity' appears rather too often and fine details are being glossed over too easily. As a result, general knowledge about details of Hindu marriage solemnization remains fairly poor; but this is not different from India either.

With regard to post-nuptial rites, and to some extent the pre-nuptial rites, I think that many British Hindus tend to ignore them as not very important and leave them to the priests, who may spend many hours in the preparation of the ritual space. The major attention is, in all cases, focused on the wedding itself, but once the couple have left the scene of the wedding and are left alone, more so when they form a new nuclear residential unit, few post-nuptial rites may be performed. Since part of the purpose of such rites, in India, is to help the settlement and adjustment of the newly-arrived woman, one should perhaps not necessarily welcome this absence of extra rituals as a good development. I have some evidence that women feel more comfortable if such rituals are performed: they have definite roles to play in stress reduction. Again, detailed research would be very useful here.

Not all indications point towards contraction and reduction of ritual complexities, then. It is in this context that I want to return to the question of ritually incorporating the registration marriage ceremony into the Hindu wedding. During the past few years, I have come across more and more evidence that this happens. I would not call it a definite trend yet, but I certainly see this differently now than a few years ago. For, rather than just going through the official registration process as an act of administration, and ignoring it altogether for ritual purposes, some Hindu families (and also some Jains) are beginning to develop new rituals out of the familiar traditional patterns for such an occasion: there may be an element of blessing ceremony, another round of gift exchanges in a ritualized form, a little video session and other elements. All this shows that the English registration ceremony is now gradually being incorporated into the Hindu wedding.

Rather than lamenting the demise of my topic under the challenge of modern secular forces, I am therefore reporting a vigorous new incarnation of the vivāha saṃskāra in 'Inglistan'. On this happy note I have to end, but not without emphasizing that sanskritists should turn to the study of such processes as I have shown here. The modern ritual developments teach us a lot about how the Sanskrit tradition may have developed and been modified historically. Clearly, a purely textual study would be unable to follow up such complex evidence, but there is much scope for the close analysis of the textual material involved in the present ritual developments. If we find, as I think we will, that the cherished notions of a philosophy-centred approach to indology and to Hinduism do not stand the test of the living reality today, it is our duty as academic specialists to develop a better understanding of how sanskritic traditions have been operating in a given society. The marvellous opportunity that the presence of so many Hindus in Britain offers us for studying such complex issues is a mixed blessing only for those who think that the Hindus of Britain will eventually 'do as the Romans do'.

My fieldwork clearly indicates that the Hindus of Britain continue to be typical Hindus in their flexible use of tradition. Mother India, even in diaspora, is as assertive as ever when it comes to incorporating novel elements into Hindu culture. In this way, in Britain today, Hindu rituals of marriage solemnization continue to be, with few exceptions, crucial and central elements of marriage law and of British Hindu culture. Without them, there is neither a complete marital union in the eyes of the community nor, it appears, an unchallengeably valid marriage in English law.

Thus, far from being phased out gradually, Hindu marriage rituals in Britain have become revitalized by new concerns and considerations. Fascinating evidence of this is now found when the legally required element of registration of the marriage is ritually built into the complex sequence of Hindu marriage rituals. By doing so, Hindus in Britain and their priestly advisors are asserting their religion's claim to universality in a surprisingly vigorous fashion. The old and well-known concept of the inclusivity of Hindu traditions is thus beautifully illustrated in its application in the modern world and, as I hope to have clearly shown here, not even the authoritative force of the British legal system is immune to such a pervasive force.

CHANGING PATTERNS IN HINDU DEATH RITUALS IN BRITAIN

Shirley Firth

In India there is considerable variety in the way death rituals are performed, depending on caste, region, and the orientation of the priests, but also influenced by growing secularization and urbanization.[1] Major cities now have electric crematoria, which have both reflected and created a shift in attitudes towards death rituals, and the advent of means of refrigeration enables people to wait more than twenty-four hours for distant relatives to arrive for a funeral. Families who have moved from rural areas to cities, or who have moved away from their own communities and extended families, may also be cut off from the religious practices common to them, and apart from the major life-cycle rites, may have little contact with priests, so there is considerable scope for innovation and change. However, there are also common patterns of death ritual, beginning with disposal of the body within twenty-four hours, and there is normally at least the possibility of finding a priest to advise and help at the time of death.

For Hindu death rituals in Britain, which are similar in principle, the changes which occur, or are perceived to occur, are due to the delay and bureaucracy surrounding cremation, to the need to return to work as soon as possible after the funeral, to inaccessibility of knowledgeable priests, and to lack of knowledge on the part of the bereaved as to how their particular gotra would perform the rituals. The pandits themselves have had to adapt to circumstances, which means truncating otherwise long rituals. Furthermore, the roles of the pandits have changed; they now combine the roles of temple priest, family purohit and mahābrāhmaṇa as well as developing, for some of them, a new pastoral role as parish priest (p. 4). They may feel obliged to undertake rituals which in India would have been undertaken by specialist priests (mahābrāhmaṇas), for which they have not been trained and which are traditionally considered degrading or polluting.

Hindu death rituals, in an ideal situation, take place over a period of time; for the purpose of comparison this period can be divided into nine stages.[2] Stage I is preparation for death, which may be seen as

1 I wish to acknowledge my gratitude to my informants in Southampton and to the following pandits in Britain who have given generously of their time, knowledge and advice: Mathoor Krishnamurti, Bharatiya Vidya Bhavan, London; Rameshbhai Mehta, Leicester; Vishnu Narayan, London; Aba Panchikar, Leicester; Madan Lal Sharma, Coventry; N. B. Shukla, Southampton. My thanks also to the following for reading the manuscript, and for their advice and encouragement: Dr. Gillian Evison, Professor Richard Gombrich, Dr. Sanjukta Gupta Gombrich, Hemant Kanitkar, Dr. Dermot Killingley, Dr. Siew-Yue Killingley, Ram Krishan, Dr. Werner Menski, Eleanor Nesbitt, Dr. Jonathan Parry.

2 Evison (1989: 5) uses a model of six stages: (1) the rites at death, the preparation of the body and the funeral procession; (2) the disposal of the body; (3) the rites concerned with the collection of bones or attention to the

part of a life-long process, or simply the last days, hours or minutes before death. Stage II involves rituals at the moment of death, and Stage III, which may overlap with it, is the preparation of the body. Stage IV is the journey to the cremation ground. Stage V is the disposal of the body, which for adults is normally by cremation;[3] Stage VI is the collection of bones (or 'ashes') on the third or fourth day; these may be deposited in a holy river immediately if possible, or await an opportunity for the chief mourner or his representative to go to the Ganges or Yamuna. Stage VII (śrāddha) involves the rites for the deceased's spirit (preta), covering the period up to the twelfth or thirteenth day, when various ceremonies enable it to take on a new spiritual body and become a pitṛ (ancestor). The first ten days of this period after death are a time of extreme impurity (sūtaka)[4] which reflects also the family's isolation and grief (śoka). Stage VIII includes ceremonies marking the end of this state. In the final Stage IX, the deceased, as an ancestor, receives daily, monthly and annual oblations. In Britain, the emphasis in this model has shifted because of changed circumstances, with an increased time lag between the death and the preparation of the body and funeral, and major alterations in the procedures of Stages III to VI. (See chart on p. 84.)

This paper is concerned primarily with Stages I to V, up to the

grave; (4) the rites for the ghost; (5) the end of mourning; (6) commemorative rites. In the present context it is useful to separate preparation for death, the rites for the dying, preparation of the body, and the journey to the cremation ground, making a total of nine stages.

3 Burial is usual in certain circumstances, e.g. for sannyasis and infants, and water burial follows death from illnesses such as smallpox, or for the very poor. Burial is also common in some communities such as the Lingāyats of South India (Evison 1989: 39).

4 *Sūtaka* (H, Gj *sūtak*) is the term most commonly used by informants, particularly those from Gujarat, and is used here as reflecting their usage. Etymologically it has to do with birth; it refers to pollution caused by birth or miscarriage, as well as to pollution in general (Monier-Williams 1899: 1240). Stevenson uses it for pollution by birth (e.g. 1920: 17) and by death (1920: 63); the latter she also calls *Mṛtaka* ['corpse'] *Sūtaka* (1920: 157). Parry's informants in Varanasi also used the term *sūtaka* for death pollution, but acknowledged that it could also be used for birth pollution (personal communication). The term *pātaka* (H, Gj *pātak*), 'sin, crime, loss of caste' (Monier-Williams 1899: 616) is applicable only to death pollution; *pāta* means 'fall' in general, and also 'death'. *Pātaka* was more commonly used by informants from Himachal Pradesh and Panjab (see also Parry 1979). *Sūtaka*, which may be originally a euphemism, is used here as reflecting the usage of most informants. Parry points out that death is, in a sense, not separable from the regeneration of the universe, and the death sacrifice also gives rise to the rebirth of the sacrificer and the sacrifice (1982: 76-77, 80f; cf Knipe 1977: 121). *Aśuddha* is another term meaning 'impure', but does not seem to be used so often. *Śoka* means 'sorrow', and the period of śoka overlaps with that of sūtaka, but will continue after sūtaka is over. Inauspiciousness is *aśubha*. (See chart on p. 84.)

funeral, in Western terms; that is, with the period from before death to the cremation of the body. While Stages I and II in India and Britain will be compared one at a time, the contrast in timing in Stages III to V means that it makes more sense to examine them consecutively in India before returning to the situation in Britain. Stages VI to IX are discussed more briefly. Comparisons between India and Britain will be based on first-hand accounts by informants in Britain and their relatives in Gujarat and Delhi, as well as their pandits, and on cremations observed in Baroda, Varanasi and Britain. With a fairly short period of fieldwork in India, however, it was only possible to obtain a limited amount of information, particularly regarding the actual content of the rituals. This discussion, therefore, will have to reflect changes as they have been observed, as they are perceived by informants, or with reference to ethnographic accounts of funeral procedures in the nineteenth and twentieth centuries. The *Preta-kalpa* contained in the *GP*, which is frequently cited as a guide, also provides a standard of comparison. For convenience, those Hindus interviewed in India will be termed *Indian informants*, while those interviewed in Britain will be termed *British informants*.

Informants

The research has taken place primarily in a small community of about a thousand Hindus in Southampton. Most of these are members of Gujarati business castes, who came here from East Africa in the late 1960s and early 1970s. There is also a small but significant number of Panjabi Hindus from brahmin and Khatri communities, many of whom came directly from India, and a few from other regions, especially Delhi, and from Fiji and Malaysia. The ages of the respondents ranged from nine to eighty years. Where possible, relatives of informants were also interviewed in India, as stated above. Where the words of informants are quoted, the abbreviations (p. 85) indicate their status, sex and approximate age.

The Hindu community in Southampton has, to some degree, been focused on the Vedic Society, which was founded in 1971 to draw people of all castes and sectarian backgrounds together, although some caste groups, such as the Lohānas, and some sectarian groups (Puṣṭimārgīs, Swāminārāyaṇ, and recently, Sathya Sāī Bābā), meet separately except for major functions and festivals (cf. Knott 1986). Initially the Society met in a school hall, then in a church hall, until a temple was built in 1984. During this time the director of the Bharatiya Vidya Bhavan in London, Sri Mathoor Krishnamurti, provided support and advice and performed various major ceremonies, such as the prāṇaprastiṣṭhā (endowing an image with life) at the opening of the new temple. In addition, priests were imported from London, Leicester or Birmingham for many ceremonies. If a pandit willing to conduct a funeral was not available when required, a senior member of the family or caste might conduct a service in the home, reciting mantras and reading from the *BhG*, and in some instances an elderly Panjabi brahmin woman did this in the undertaker's chapel of rest. In the early days a local Sikh also led some funerals. The first resident pandit was appointed in 1986, but left after the expiry of a two-year contract; currently there is a śāstrī, who, after studying Sanskrit in Baroda, worked as a temple priest in East Africa before coming to Britain in 1988. Although he conducts most funerals, local Ārya Samājī families may still invite their own priest because they wish to perform the final havan immediately after the cremation which the local pandit will not countenance during the time of maximum impurity (cf. pp. 77f).

The difficulties which Hindus in many parts of Britain experience with regard to funerals has led some communities to produce an order of service, and in 1987 the National Council of Hindu Temples published a standardized one in English, Gujarati, and Hindi with Sanskrit. The pandits interviewed for this study were very critical of it on the grounds that it did not contain enough of the proper rituals (cf. p. 82) for the release of the soul, but recognized its usefulness when a 'learned brahmin' was not available.

At the time of death there is great solidarity shown in the community, but many traditions are based on family or caste, so that people will turn to their own relatives—often in India or East Africa—for advice, or failing that, to caste peers locally. Thus a bereaved Panjabi Ārya Samāj family from East Africa will receive help and advice from similar families, but there will also be support from Panjabi neighbours of different traditions.

Stage I: Preparation for death

Preparation for death is a gradual process throughout an individual's life. At one level, as Stevenson points out,

> Through all his rites and rejoicing, a Hindu has been preparing for death, for...the thread that strings all the ceremonies together is the imperative desire that the funeral offerings should be perfectly performed.

At a second level, the observation of his dharma throughout his life, through proper religious, social and ethical behaviour, will engender enough merit to ensure a felicitous rebirth (Stevenson 1920: 136). This will also, together with good karma from his previous lives, ensure a long life. At a third level, preparation involves a process of detachment from worldly attachments and a turning to spiritual matters in the hope of liberation, or mokṣa. This is enshrined in the ideal of the four āśramas or stages of life (student, householder, forest-dweller and ascetic), in which the householder, having produced sons and grandsons, withdraws with his wife into the forest and eventually ends his days as a sannyāsin (Stevenson 1920: 139; Basham 1967: 159-60; Brockington 1981: 92). Many informants in both India and Britain referred to this ideal, describing relatives who had gradually withdrawn emotionally and mentally, if not physically, in order to concentrate on reading the scriptures, prayer and meditation.

Preparation for death in India

In practical terms, there are many preparations which can be made as death approaches. Business affairs need to be set in order and matters of inheritance sorted out. Last-minute instructions have to be given to the family and marriages arranged for unmarried daughters and nieces. The person who is spiritually prepared for death may have foreknowledge of the day and even the time he will die (Parry 1982: 82). Several informants described a relative who had called all his family together and ordered his own preparations: 'He told them to clean the floor, took his bath, lay on the floor and died chanting mantras' (GjBrM70: cf. Madan 1987: 123; Firth 1989: 70). Sometimes, without specifically saying why, they had written letters (seen retrospectively as farewells) to close relatives, and often remarks were made indicating they were ready for death and wanted to go in peace. An elderly Sindhi woman had a suit (salvār qamīz) dipped in Ganges water prepared in advance. When she felt death was approaching she sent her son out of the house so she could be alone, had a bath, put on the suit, and lay on her bed chanting 'Rām, Rām'. Her nurse, in alarm, called the doctor, who arrived just before she died, and she said, 'You won't have to bathe and change me because we've already done that, haven't we?' Such deaths, after a long life, are thought of as 'good deaths' (su-mṛtyu) or, in the case of individuals who are wholly conscious of impending death and enter it willingly, 'willed deaths' (icchā-mṛtyu) or conscious death (caitanya-mṛtyu).

> Having previously predicted the time of his going and set all his affairs in order, he gathers his sons about him and—by an effort of concentrated will—abandons life. He is not said to die, but to relinquish his body (Parry 1982: 82; cf. Madan 1987: 125ff).

The good death is characterized by the right place (sthāna) on the banks of the Ganges or on the ground at home rather than in hospital; the time (kāla), which should be astrologically correct, and the personal state of the dying individual. The converse is a bad death (ku-mṛtyu) or untimely death (akāla-mṛtyu), exemplified by premature death from violence or by accident, or death at any age from diseases such as cholera or leprosy. This is the death

> for which the deceased cannot be said to have prepared himself. It is said that 'he did not die his own death' (Parry 1982: 83; cf. Firth 1989: 69).

Because of the importance of dying at home, several Hindu doctors said that they made provision for a dying person to be taken home to die. As one of them said, 'We do not consider hospital is a very holy place' (GjBrF35). However, two other doctors, a Bengali brahmin in Calcutta and a Parsi in Pune, said that they were reluctant to inform patients and relatives who were not already aware of the fact that death was imminent, for fear the family might create a scene in the hospital, or the patient might be disturbed, thus placing the efficiency of the hospital, and possibly the immediate comfort of the patient, above the longer-term religious requirements of the patient and family. The value of dying at home, in addition to the psychological advantage of being surrounded by the family, lies in the help and support the family can give in facilitating a good death by enabling the individual to lie on the floor, to have appropriate readings or mantras, and to have the correct procedures at the last minute (pp. 59-61).

As death approaches, a general act of penance (sarva-prāyaścitta) should be performed with the help of the family purohit. Although the custom was said to be dying out, a number of Gujarati and Panjabi informants described five gifts (pañca-dāna), including land (bhūmi-dāna), clothes, grains, a cow or cow and calf (go-dāna), and money, which should be given to brahmins, to the poor, and to worthy institutions by the dying individual, or failing that, by his or her son or closest male relative (Stevenson 1920: 140; Kane 1953: 184; cf. Dubois 1906: 482; *GP* 2, 4, 3-9; 2, 36, 23-32; Planalp 1956: 598; Monier-Williams 1884: 296; Quayle et al. 1980: 9). The father of one informant had a dharmaśālā for pilgrims built at Rishikesh. The cow, referred to as the Vaitaraṇī cow, enables the ātman to cross the terrible river of death, the Vaitaraṇī Nadī (Pandey 1969: 420). Some Gujarati families bring the cow into the house, and pour water and milk over its tail. The dying person then has to hold the tail before presenting the animal to the brahmin, thus ensuring that the ātman will be able to hold it while crossing the river (cf. Madan 1987: 134; Planalp 1956: 598; Stevenson 1920: 141; Kane 1953: 183; Evison 1989: 12-14). Nowadays a small silver substitute, or its full value, is sometimes offered instead, accompanied by a go-dāna saṃkalpa. This ritual statement of intention, with the gift of a substitute of equal or lesser value, obtains the same merit as the gift of an actual cow (Stevenson 1920: 78). The gifts, either before or at death, ease the suffering of the dying person as well as giving him or her merit. According to a brahmin informant in Varanasi, it is the mahābrāhmaṇa (funeral priest) who receives these gifts because the gifts are 'heavy' with the sin of the dying person (Kaushik 1976: 270). Elsewhere, informants said the pre-death gifts could be given to a 'perfect' or learned brahmin—usually the family priest (*GP* 2, 4, 7-8).

Preparation for death in Britain

Many British Hindus referred to the concept of a good death. It is not just a question of acquiring good karma, but of being close to God, so that at the time of death the mind is fixed on him, and one is ready to go. If one is already spiritually prepared and detached from material things, then a sudden death will not matter so much (Mahatma Gandhi's death often being given as an example). As with Indian informants, there are a number of accounts of relatives who knew they were dying and made preparations accordingly. A Panjabi woman described the death of her mother in Delhi. At a hundred and three, she was able to walk without a stick and thread a needle without glasses. She knew she was going to die, and went into the house, calling her daughter and grandson. She asked them to prepare a dīvā (lamp) to show her the way to God. She asked her grandson to put her head on his lap, and told her daughter not to weep, as she was going to God, and the daughter's tears would make a river for her to cross (cf. Vaitāraṇī Nadī (pp. 57, 60).

While it is acknowledged that it is important to perform an act of penance and make reparation before death, no informants have mentioned the necessity of a formal ritual in the presence of a purohit or of the need to offer gifts before death, although gifts after death (including, for some families, the silver calf for the pandit) are seen as very important. All the priests interviewed regarded the rituals before death as important, especially the gifts, and said the pandits should be willing to go several days before death if necessary, but that they have rarely, if ever, been called upon to go. A Gujarati Pandit said,

> This time should be ātur samay [literally 'impatient time'], the time when a person should be eager to go back, like a child eager to go back to his mother after school. He has sent us to do certain work and he waits for us.

He said the gifts should involve bhūmi-dāna and go-dāna in order to compensate for omissions, as well as making confession for wrongs done. There should be Viṣṇu Pūjā and mantras according to texts such as *Karmakāṇḍa* by Sri Naturam Sharma, but he acknowledged the problems of realizing these goals in Britain. Another pandit, from Bihar, had spent time reading to a dying friend, but had not performed rituals at the end because he had been unable to be present.

Stage II: The moment of death

Since there is often a fluid process of activity from the preparation to the moment of death and the activities which follow, with some possibly overlapping others in time, the divisions may seem artificial; they are made here for convenience. Hindus in India and Britain believe it is very important for the individual to be placed on the floor just before death if possible—with Ganges water and tulsi[5] in the mouth. It is vital that the dying person should have the thought of God in the mind (Parry 1982: 83); to this end the family

5 Both tulsi (tulasī, basil) and Ganges water enable one to reach mokṣa. According to the *Pūjā-ratnākara*, 'one dying in a garden of *tulasī* plants or with Tulasī leaf placed in his mouth at the time of death attains *mokṣa* even if guilty of crores of sins' (Kane 1953: 187). Dying by the Ganges has the same effect (Parry 1982: 74). Dying with Ganges water in the mouth is the next best thing, and also has a purificatory effect (Stevenson 1920: 143). Immersing the bones and ashes in the Ganges also leads to mokṣa; hence the great efforts among British Hindus to get this done.

should assist by reading the scriptures or chanting the name of God or favourite mantras.

The moment of death in India

Ritually, the dying person should be purified by bathing and drinking or being sprinkled with pañca-gavya, the five products of a cow. Some Indian informants said the death should take place outside, on the ground, or at least on the earth of a courtyard (Parry 1982: 82); others said it should take place on the floor, or the body should be placed on the floor or taken outside the moment death occurred (Kaushik 1976: 270-1, fn 276; Padfield 1896: 194-6; Stevenson 1920: 142; Kane 1953: 184). The earth or floor should be prepared with cowdung and darbha grass, and sesame (*GP* 2, 2, 7-8; Evison 1989: 198). According to the scriptures the dying person should be placed 'on a cleansed spot on sandy soil...in proximity to the three fires, or if he preserves only one, near it, viz., the domestic fire', implying that the death should take place indoors (Pandey 1969: 246 citing *AGS* 4, 1; Kane 1953: 182 citing *KGS* 80, 3). Ārya Samājīs who perform havan daily will thus prefer to die on the floor in the proximity of the sacred fire. According to Padfield, in South India death out of doors was only important if the death occurred during the inauspicious periods, since this would be so polluting it would involve abandoning the house for several months (1895: 195-6). If the death occurs indoors the doors should be opened, as open spaces 'allow the ātmā to merge with Brahman more readily' (VrBr42). Evison has shown that this practice is widespread throughout India, and is legitimated by the sūtra literature and *GP*, although the reasons given may differ. Usually the reason given by informants for placing the person on the floor or ground was to be 'near 'Mother Earth', 'to allow the ātmā to escape more easily', or 'to allow the person to breathe more easily'. The concept of earth as a mother protecting the dead is an ancient one, going back to *ṚV* 10, 18, 10-11 (cf. also *TS* 1, 4, 40; Evison 1989: 197, 305). According to a Bihari pandit, death outside is a sign of freedom, indicated by the loosening of all knots in the clothing, whereas death under a roof signifies bondage, as does death on a bed (see next paragraph). Furthermore, death on the ground signifies the return of the ātman and the body to the elements from which they came. The ground has to be purified with cowdung and sesame, and according to the *GP*, a protective circle has to be drawn around the space to prevent 'foul spirits' entering the corpse (2, 2, 7ff). Contact with the earth may be compared to holding the tail of the Vaitaraṇī cow (p. 57 above); both the earth and the cow are symbols of universal motherhood for Hindus, and *go* 'cow' can also mean 'earth'.

The *GP*, taking a more negative position, states that to die on a bed is dangerous because ghosts and spirits can attack the deceased, who will then become a permanent ghost himself unless a remedial ritual called the *nārāyaṇa bali* is performed (*GP* 2, 4, 104-12; 2, 10; 15, 6; 29, 9). Dubois' account suggests that the dying brahmin, if he expires on a bed, 'would be obliged to carry it with him wherever he went, which, it may easily be supposed, would be very inconvenient' (1906: 499; Padfield 1895: 194-6). Planalp's informants said that the charpoy (bed) was impure and those who died on it could be caught in a web of future lives (1956: 59). Kaushik points out that the thing most Hindus adhere to most strictly is to die on the ground rather than on one's bed (1976: 270-1, 283); as can be seen below (p. 63), this concern remains important for Hindus in Britain, although it is rarely possible in a hospital setting.

Most informants said the body must be laid with the head to the north, as stated in the *GP*, although the latter also allows the head to the east (*GP* 2, 32, 88; Stevenson 1920: 14). A London-based pandit said that Gujaratis place the head to the north but that elsewhere it is placed to the south. Since a body with the feet to the south may be said to face south, these are two ways of applying the same principle, that the south is the direction of Yama and the pitṛs (cf. Pandey 1969: 246):

> Being in the right direction enables Yama Rājā to swoop up and grab you as he comes up from the south. (PjKhM)

Many educated informants said that the north-south orientation allows the magnetic currents of the earth to pass through the body and ease the passing of the ātman, but a pandit described this as 'scientific mumbo jumbo'.

Immediately before or after death, Ganges water (or Yamuna water in the case of Puṣṭimārgīs) and tulsi leaves are placed in the mouth: a small pot of sacred water is kept ready in the house, and families will have a tulsi plant—or ready access to one—even if they are Śaivite. Gold, which should be put in after death (p. 64 below) may also be placed in the mouth before death (cf. Stevenson 1920: 143), and one informant claimed that forcing a coin into the mouth of a dying patient sometimes actually choked him (Evison 1989: 8).

Most informants spoke of the importance of the family being present even if the dying person wanted to be alone, so that they could say goodbye, ask forgiveness, and make arrangements for property, and so that he could 'speak kind words'. It is also necessary for the family to help the dying person fix his mind on God, because the last thoughts determine one's status in the next life (*BhG* 8, 5-6; *ChUp* 2, 14, 1; Madan 1987: 124; Kane 1953: 185-6; Monier-Williams 1884: 297). However, it is imperative for people present to be otherwise quiet, and only read the *BhG* or sing bhajans. An eighty-four-year-old Panjabi brahmin said that only the pictures of the gods should be present; any people who were there should chant *BhG* 18 because if they thought of worldly things the soul would wander. An elderly Gujarati said,

> If you find me dying don't talk because it will draw my soul back. I don't want to hear any human voices except the sound of 'Rām, Rām'.

Tears can create an even bigger river to cross (p. 57). An elderly Puṣṭimārgī Patel said that when his grandfather died at ninety-nine, his grandson asked him whether he should read the *BhG* or some

Puṣṭimārgī books by Vallabhācārya, and he said, 'The *Gītā* has gone through my mind throughout my life so you need not do it.' Having called his sons and daughters the previous day, he announced that he would be leaving this world the next morning at 8 a.m. and asked, 'Do you want me to carry a message to the next world? To whom?' and laughed very loudly. The value of having at least some relatives present was that if the dying person was unconscious or in a great deal of pain they could help fix his mind on God by singing bhajans, chanting the *BhG*, especially chapter 15, and saying the Gāyatrī mantra. At the point of death it is helpful to say in the dying person's ear 'Rām', 'oṃ', or 'śrī kṛṣṇaḥ śaraṇaṃ mama' ('Lord Kṛṣṇa is my refuge') if Vaiṣṇavite, or 'oṃ namaḥ śivāya' ('Homage to Śiva') if Śaivite.

The moment of death in Britain

British Hindus have similar attitudes regarding the moment of death. Death should take place on the floor if possible, and the family should be present (cf. pp. 56 and 60). However, since most deaths are either unexpected—a number of instances have been heart attacks while out of the house—or take place in hospital, this is very difficult to put into practice, which causes considerable anxiety:

> A lot of people die in hospital and [we can't] put the bodies on the floor...a lot of us families are very shy to follow very strictly—we feel out of place, like a Muslim praying towards Mecca on the factory floor. (PjBrM40)

It is vital to have the family present, so that arrangements can be made and proper goodbyes said. Lack of understanding and communication here cause more distress than anything else:

> I kept on saying, 'Is there anything to worry about?', and they said, 'Nothing, we'll take care of him. Pneumonia is nothing nowadays.'...and at 3 a.m. there was a phone call...and this doctor said, 'Your father has passed away.'...If he had known he would have had everything done. He always told us, 'I'm not scared of dying...I'm not worried at all, as long as I know what is happening'...He would have prayed...in his last time, but really he would have worried about us...He would have had a bit of strength: 'At least my family's with me at my last time.' If we had had the slightest idea we would have sat in the waiting-room all night...I said [to the nurse], 'Did my father say anything at the end?' and she said, 'Oh, do you expect people when they die to say things in your religion?'...and I said, 'I just want to know what his last words were.'...And she said, 'Oh, I didn't know that you'd have expected him to say anything', as if it was something really strange and out of this world that a person dying would say anything. (PjKhF14)

Last words are very important, especially those of someone who has died a good death, which are spoken about and remembered for years afterwards (Madan 1987: 124). However, it is not just the psychological aspect which matters. As has been seen, the dying person must have his or her thoughts fixed on God, and if the family are not there to see to this, there is no one to help a patient who may be in pain or unconscious:

> In hospital, when someone is near to death then he must have his next-of-kin with him. When people know that he is near to death we start reciting the *Gītā* or religious books. Obviously, we must be told [that the person is dying] rather than keeping the news away and only being told after the death has happened. I know it's not easy to say, 'Look, he is going to die.' It's easier to say, 'He's all right, nothing to worry about.' (PjBrM45)

If rituals are not performed properly the survivors and possibly the whole extended family may be affected, often for a long time. The giving of Ganges water at the point of death enables the dying person 'to be happy and reach the happy abode', as one pandit puts it. But, he adds,

> If the moment is missed it can be done immediately afterwards and [one can] offer two or three grains of rice, the most symbolic food we can offer, with tīl and gingely oil. It is said in the śāstras that the departed soul is a conveyance, a vehicle, so we sprinkle and throw sīsūm on the body because the moment a man dies his soul departs and he can reach only through this means, this vehicle. (KanPt)

However, some informants believe that if Ganges water is not given before death it can have devastating effects on the whole family. An elderly aunt of a Gujarati informant was dying of cancer in an intensive care unit in hospital. The doctors, thinking death was imminent, switched off the life-support machine, but refused to allow the relatives present to give her Ganges water, on the grounds that it might choke her and the shock might kill her. The consequence of this has affected the whole family for ten years, and no auspicious ceremonies can be performed without performing penances because she died without water, 'and therefore her soul is still not free and her family is not free...and all the children born into this family will have to do these penances for seven generations, just to free her soul'. The only way to resolve this would be to perform a very expensive penance, a saptāha, involving the whole extended family, over a period of more than seven days, in the hope of nourishing and satisfying the soul.[6] The importance of doing the ritual correctly appears to outweigh the immediate need of the patient for comfort and peace.

6 A saptāha consists of seven days of readings, during which a hundred sādhus are fed, which costs about £70 in India. In the UK, this would be replaced by feasting brahmins, friends and relatives, which would cost nearer £800, according to the family quoted here. It is not the same as nārāyaṇa bali (pp. 59, 79), which is for violent deaths.

For the British Hindu, then, the rituals at the point of death do not require a pandit, but ideally involve dying on the floor in the presence of the family, with tulsi and Ganges water in the mouth, and with the name of God on the lips and in the heart. While older people remember the rituals as performed in India, these are regarded as dispensable in the present circumstances, but there is anxiety if the basic observances are made impossible. This can create obvious problems in a hospital setting, as there may be tensions between the need to fulfil obligations on behalf of the departing soul (and secure the subsequent safety of the family), and the comfort of the patient as perceived by the medical staff. A further problem can be created by a demand for large numbers of relatives chanting around a bed in a ward, as this can upset other patients. It can also upset a patient who may not be aware that death is imminent, which is why some doctors in India are hesitant to inform the family and patient that this is likely (cf. pp. 56f). Nevertheless, hospitals in Britain are slowly changing, and some will permit the patient to have a mattress on the floor in a single room, so that the family can be present.

Stage III: Preparation of the body in India

In India, Stages III, IV and V are part of a ritual process which forms a continuum from the moment of death: the preparation of the body, offerings of piṇḍas in the home, the journey to the cremation ground and the cremation itself. Normally these will all take place within twenty-four hours of the death: the same day if it is still daylight and the chief mourner can get there, or the following day (Stevenson 1920: 144). These stages will be discussed together before looking at the situation in Britain.

Many of the things which should be done before death, such as placing the person on the floor and giving Ganges water and tulsi, can be done the moment a person has died. A lamp is lit and placed near the head. The family may turn to experienced relatives to find out the correct procedures regarding preparation of the body and the ritual journey. Often it is elderly uncles and aunts who are called upon to give information. A distinction is made between kulācāra (family traditions) and deśācāra (regional traditions). Another distinction is sometimes made between śāstrika (what is perceived to be correct according to the śāstras or the brahmanical tradition) and laukika or lokācāra (local or family traditions). It does not seem to be usual for a purohit to go to the home except in the case of brahmin clients, but he may go to the cremation ground.

The most important functionary from this moment onwards is the chief mourner, who has to perform the rites associated with the cremation itself, the piṇḍa ceremonies on the day of the cremation, subsequent ceremonies up to the thirteenth day, or whenever the mourning is concluded, and also the annual śrāddha (p. 79). Ideally this functionary is a son who is old enough to have had the upanayana (the sacred thread ceremony); but he may be a brother, father, or male cousin. He may also be an adopted son, although the deceased man's brothers might object if there is property at stake. (Because of the problems attending the division of property at death, it is common for a man without a son to adopt a nephew as a son.) In some cases a daughter-in-law or wife may perform the rites if the son is away, and an unmarried Nair woman informant herself performed the ceremony for her father, despite objections from the community. The chief mourner should be someone whose own preta, after death, will join those of the deceased's ancestors, or if the deceased is a married woman, her husband's ancestors, since she is no longer part of her father's lineage but has joined that of her husband (Dumont 1983: 6ff). A son-in-law should not normally perform the ceremonies for his father-in-law, since he is not a member of the deceased's lineage, although in the absence of anyone else he may (cf. Kane 1953: 220). An informant explained that the ātman may return to the house in order to be born again in the same lineage, and would be confused by rites conducted by someone who was not part of that lineage (GjBrM).

In some Gujarati communities, if a married woman dies and her husband intends to remarry, or his family thinks he should, he will not act as chief mourner at the cremation of his wife, and may signal his intention by tearing off a strip of her red covering cloth and leaving it in the doorway.

Respondents from all regions mentioned a gold or silver coin (pavitṛ 'purifier') in the mouth, either immediately death occurs or after the body has been dressed (Stevenson 1920: 143). Most said this was to pay the ferryman while crossing the river of death (Vaitaraṇī Nadī) (p. 57), but a Gujarati brahmin said it was a germicidal agent, and a Delhi brahmin said it used to be done to ensure rebirth in an affluent family. Five substances (pañcāmṛta): honey, sugar, milk, ghi and curd; and five metals: gold, silver, copper, brass and nickel may also be placed in the mouth (*GP* 2, 15, 6-11).

The body is bathed and dressed by relatives and friends of the same sex and caste. The *GP* (2, 4, 44) states that this should be done immediately. It is bathed in Ganges or Yamuna water and dressed in new clothes, which in some instances have been bought in advance and dipped in Ganges or Yamuna water. There is considerable variation according to caste and region as to the treatment of the body. Generally a man will be dressed or wrapped in a dhoti, although a Rajput said the body was not really dressed, but just covered in pieces of red, yellow and white silk, with no knots, which were gradually removed as far as modesty permitted, as the body was covered with cowdung at the pyre. They were then given to the attendants (cf. Padfield 1896: 199; p. 68 below). A woman who has the good fortune to die before her husband will be dressed in her wedding sari, and if her husband dies first, he may be covered with her wedding sari, or with a red cloth (GjPt). A widow will be dressed in white, an unmarried woman in white or red, depending on her age (Panalp 1956: 599; Kane 1953: 212; Dubois 1906: 484; Quayle 1980: 10; Stevenson 1920: 144). The thumbs and toes are tied with a holy thread of seven colours called *nālā chadī*

because a dying person feels tense and if the two toes are not tied when the

> soul leaves, the person may die with the legs apart. It is very difficult to join the two legs together. (GjP1F48; cf. Gopal 1959: 355; Evison 1989: 21)

It is placed on a ladder-like stretcher, and may be decorated with garlands and ornaments, and if the deceased had been wealthy, two pearls may be put on the eyes (Jackson and Killingley 1988: 91). Four coconuts may be tied to the corners of the stretcher, which, according to a Gujarati Patel woman, symbolize the four ambassadors of Yama who come to carry the dead. She said that if the deceased is a kṣatriya, 'the arms are arranged above the head with the palms up', representing the status and wealth they received at birth. Brahmins in Gujarat are usually tied on to a single pole rather than a stretcher, with just two coconuts tied on the pole (Stevenson 1920: 146).

The corpse has an ambiguous status as being both highly inauspicious and auspicious (Evison 1989: 5). All the individuals in the house are now impure, according to my informants, and will be for at least ten days, although, according to the pandits interviewed by Parry in Varanasi, pollution begins after the kapāla kriyā (1982: 79). At the same time the corpse is being prepared as a sacrifice to Agni, and is treated with great respect: 'It is treated as a god/goddess in the house and circumambulated in the auspicious direction (with the right shoulder to the corpse), while the mourners at the same time are wearing their threads in the inauspicious direction [i.e., over the right shoulder]' (Evison 1989: 24, 26; cf. Das 1976: 253; Stevenson 1920: 143f; Planalp 1956: 602); the circumambulation may be reversed at the pyre (Stevenson 152). Various Gujarati informants said the body was regarded as Viṣṇu, Lakṣmī, Śiva (Das 1976) or Kṛṣṇa. It has to be guarded against objects and animals (Das (1976; Stevenson 1920: 145) and cannot be touched by anyone outside the caste (Pandey 1969: 248; *MS* 5, 104). Carrying the body is 'a sacred affair' (GjBrM35; PjKhM45), and the chief mourner, who in some areas will have had his head shaved by the barber, bathes and puts on a white dhoti but does not wear either shoes or shirt (Das 1976: 253; Stevenson 1920: 148). In other areas his head will be shaved at the cremation ground prior to or after the cremation (Padfield 1896: 201; Planalp 1956: 606). The family then circumambulates the body from one to seven times:

> You have to walk around the body four times clockwise with millet and sesame seeds in the palm, sprinkling it and saying 'śrī kṛṣṇaḥ śaraṇaṃ mama; I yield to thy feet, Lord Kṛṣṇa.' After the four revolutions the person doing them will touch the feet, and others will, in turn. [The dead person] is like a devatā, almost a god, so revolving around four times is like a pilgrimage of four dhāmas.[7] It is the person, not the body [you are honouring]. This is not to protect the soul but to discharge an emotional debt. Before dying we might still owe a person and we want to pay that

7 *dhāman* 'abode (of a god)'; cf. Gonda 1967. The four dhāmans are the four points of the compass, and also (since a sacred place is a microcosm of the universe) four points around a place of pilgrimage which are visited in turn by pilgrims, or by an image carried in procession (cf. Eck 1983: 288-90).

debt (GjPlM; cf. Das 1976: 253; Stevenson 1920: 145).

For the mourners the circumambulations seem to have several functions. The informant above saw them, or the touching of the feet which follows them, primarily as discharging a debt (ṛṇa), which would be especially important if the deceased is a parent or grandparent (*TS* 6, 3, 10, 5; Malamoud 1983: 26ff). If the corpse is like a god, then the circumambulations would also seem to have the same function as in the case of an image, and thus be associated with darśana, in which the mourners receive the blessing of the deity by being 'in his sight'. Indeed, the term *darśana* has been used by British informants (GjPlM30; PjBrM45). At the pyre they have the purpose of creating a boundary around the corpse, and this may also be a factor here--a boundary which protects the newly-released soul (preta) and the body from ghosts and the mourners from the preta, which may still be attached to the family. Finally, it may be a rite of separation of psychological significance to the mourners.

Stage IV: Piṇḍadāna and the journey to the cremation ground in India

According to many Indian informants and textual sources, piṇḍas (balls of rice, wheat or barley) should be placed at the place of death and at various strategic locations on the way to the cremation ground, although others said this was no longer done or were not sure about it. Most brahmin informants said there should be six piṇḍas offered, beginning at the home and ending at the pyre (Kane 1953: : 219; Planalp 1956: 600ff; Quayle 1980: 10), but the *GP* specifies five, the sixth to be offered when the bones are collected on the third or fourth day (*GP* 2, 4, 48f; 15, 30ff; 35, 33f; cf. Parry 1985: 615ff). They have the dual function of protecting the ghost from dangerous spirits, and of satisfying it and enabling it to become fit to be a pitṛ (*GP* 2, 4, 61):

> If a person dies with wishes unfulfilled he will become a ghost so won't get mokṣa or reincarnation, so the piṇḍa guarantees it won't wander. The six piṇḍas are for six evil entities, who have to be satisfied, so they won't harass the dead person. (GjPt)

These are the first of a series of sixteen piṇḍas, the remaining ten being in theory offered, one each day, for ten days, to enable the newly-released preta to form a new body, although many people offer all ten on the tenth day (Stevenson 1920: 149; cf. p. 79 below). The chief mourner, having been shaved, bathed, and wearing[8] his sacred

8 Pt Mathoor Krishnamurthi and Hemant Kanitkar state that the thread should be worn only as a mālā, i.e. as a rosary or necklace, when making offerings to the deceased, and certainly at the pyre. According to Parry's informants in Varanasi, the thread should be worn over the left shoulder at the pyre, before circumambulating the pyre with the right shoulder to it. Cf. Stevenson (1920: 229); Kane (1941: 287f).

thread in the inauspicious direction over his right shoulder, should offer the first, the sthāna piṇḍa, on the spot where the person died (Evison 1989: 26; Planalp 1956: 601). The family purohit usually directs this, although when available a specialist priest (mahābrāhmaṇa or acarāj) may be called. Subsequent piṇḍas are offered at the doorway (dvāra piṇḍa), and may be offered in the courtyard (tṛtīya piṇḍa) or at the edge of the village, halfway to the cremation ground at a halt or at the crossroads, outside the cremation ground (viśrāma piṇḍa) and at the cremation ground. The last piṇḍa is the śmasāna or śava piṇḍa, offered for the kṣetrapāla, sometimes identified with Mahābhairava (Śiva), the protector of the area, to ask his permission for the cremation (VrBrM42; cf. Evison 1989: 46, 216, 325), although a Bihari pandit said that in Bihar the offerings were made after the cremation.

All the Indian informants stressed the importance of the journey to the cremation ground, which has to be on foot, with male members of the family and caste peers carrying the body as a sacred duty, although it was mentioned with some outrage that nowadays bodies are sometimes taken by jeep or ambulance to the cremation ground. The chief mourner may assist in the carrying of the body or he may precede the body, carrying a brass or clay pot, bound with vines, containing fire from the domestic hearth (GjPt; GjVM32), or water (PjBrM65; UPKhM60; cf. *GP*2, 15, 12f; Padfield 1898: 198; Stevenson 1920: 146; Shastri 1963: 28; Pandey 1969: 248). The brass pot is later given to the mahābrāhmaṇa or officiant and the clay pot broken at some stage (pp. 69-71).

Only men attend the cremations, particularly in Gujarat, but there are changes in cities like Delhi, where one cremation ground has a stand for women (PjKhF), and a number of Panjabi informants in Britain spoke of women attending cremations in cities like Chandigarh. Normally women follow as far as the edge of the village or the crossroads and then return to bathe and clean the house. In some villages, professional mourners may still be called, but the practice is dying out. The women are expected to weep and wail (which informs the neighbourhood about the death), while the men are expected to keep much more in control of their emotions, and be 'stone-hearted', although they too may weep (cf. p. 79; Stevenson 1920: 145; Madan 1987: 135).

Although there was some disagreement, most said that the body had to leave the house feet first, and after a halt outside the cremation ground at a special place with a platform (the viśrāma), it was turned so it could enter the ground head first (Stevenson 1920: 149). At the visrāma the chief mourner may make a number of rounds sprinkling water from the clay pot, which is then broken on a step at the foot of the platform. This was understood to symbolize the release of the ātman (UPKhM) and the breaking of the relationship with the person (PjKhM62; cf. pp. 69f).

Stage V: The cremation in India

Three cremation grounds (śmaśāna) were visited in India, one of which included an electric crematorium. The Baroda ground was located in a beautiful garden, with an electric crematorium, of a tasteful modern design, at some distance from the open pyres. The cheapest cremations took place on pyres built in concrete pits; there were also iron crib-like structures, which presumably burned faster but used more wood, and an elaborate roofed structure for those who could afford it, which provided shade from the sun. The electric crematorium made provision for rituals by means of a platform just outside the cremator, allowing the mourners to circumambulate it. At the ghats in Chandod, near Baroda, where three sacred rivers join, and in Varanasi, pyres were built on the river bank in a manner more typical of village India.

While the details of the cremation procedures vary somewhat—for example, whether there should be wood or cowdung for the fire; whether there should be clockwise or anti-clockwise circumambulations; and the number of piṇḍas to be offered—it can be seen from the accounts given mainly by Gujarati and Panjabi informants that there are common principles and patterns: at least one piṇḍa is given as an offering; circumambulations are made around the pyre with water and fire; and there is a symbolic if not actual breaking of the skull (Evison 1989: 52).

According to a description by a Panjabi brahmin, on arrival at the ghat the chief mourner cleans an area with cowdung (this is not done in Varanasi, presumably because the place is already so sacred) and then washes the first piece of wood with water and puts it in place. The rest of the pyre is made by friends and relatives who know how, although in Varanasi the Doms, an untouchable caste who look after the the cremation ghats, may prepare and tend the fire (Eck 1983: 249), so that it is unnecessary to carry fire to the cremation ground, as the fires are always burning. Latecomers who have not been to the house may offer a red cloth (tali), the last cloth for the corpse, which is a meritorious action for the donor. The body may have further cleansing (Padfield 1896: 199; Shastri 1963: 29), and may have some clothing and the covering cloths removed, which are then given to the śmaśāna attendants (Padfield 1896), although at Varanasi I saw the wrapped bodies, tied to the stretcher, being burned as they were (Eck 1983: 249). In some traditions the face is uncovered for a last farewell, before being covered with ghi and possibly Ganges water, which may be sprinkled on the body as well. The body is then placed on the pyre. It is at this point that the last piṇḍa is offered (cf. p. 67). It may be placed on the ground at the head of the body 'to show the way to the soul', or on its folded hands or stomach.

The chief mourner has to circumambulate the body, and again there is considerable variation as to how this is done. If he has not already done it at the entrance to the ground (p. 68), he may circumambulate the body, carrying a clay pot of water before the fire is lit. A hole is made in the pot for the first pradakṣina, a second hole for the second and a third hole for the third. This has the purpose of enabling the soul to rise upwards in the direction it is supposed to go; of purifying it (Evison 1989: 53); of protecting it from the dangers of the cremation ground; and of creating a boundary between the living and the dead, thus symbolizing both separation and farewell (Padfield 1896: 200; Srinivas 1965: 151). If the chief mourner has brought fire from the domestic hearth in a pot, he may carry this around prior to lighting the fire, and at Varanasi I saw brands of burning grass either being taken around the body or waved around it. The pot may be broken now, or after the cremation. This seems to have the symbolic meaning of the skull being broken, as some informants say this enables the last remaining airs in the skull to be freed (cf. fn 10 on p. 71). In some communities the breaking of the pot is accompanied by a shout; in others this occurs later:

> Many people shout when the fire is being lit, to make the chief mourner cry and also to scare away evil spirits. After that, when doing kriyā you are not supposed to cry, but at this stage you should cry so as not to get too depressed. (GjBrM)

A number of informants said that the circumambulations here had to be clockwise (pradakṣina):

> I move around thee, please forgive me. May whatever sin I have committed in this life and the previous life be forgiven by doing this pradakṣina (BihPt; cf. Padfield 1898: 200; Parry 1982: 78).

Other informants said emphatically they should be anti-clockwise (cf. Das 1977: 122; Parry 1982: 79; Kaushik 1976: 277; Evison 1989: 30). A knowledgeable Panjabi brahmin from Varanasi, who, incidentally, belonged to a Tantric sect, said that the chief mourner should make five or seven 'half' circumambulations

> which should not cross at the feet. Never make a complete circle because the feet of the corpse are related to śakti, so, without the soul, body—śab [śava 'corpse']—can't cross over to become Śiva. The power is gone.[9]

The chief mourner has to give the fire, which is lit with camphor, burning cowdung from the domestic fire, and kuśa grass or wood, and he may take the burning brand round the body. (At one cremation I observed in Varanasi, the chief mourner just stood where he was and waved a long bunch of burning grass around the body.) As the fire is lit he prays

> to the god Agni to arrange that the dead body doesn't suffer as an evil spirit and wander around. Agni is the purest of all. Agni is also the giver of pain, caused by Agni. The revolutions with water are to relieve the pain. (GjPu)

Halfway through the cremation, in many but not all regions, the skull is broken with a bamboo (kapāla-kriyā, literally 'skull action')

9 Similar incomplete circumambulations are made round a liṅga, stopping at the line marked by the spout of the yoni. The feet of the corpse, according to the informant, are related to śakti, and the yoni is also śakti. Word-play over *śava* 'corpse' and *Śiva* is part of the Sākta tradition.

because 'some śvāsas (airs) remain in the uppermost region of the head', which have to be released to enter the five elements, the pañca-tattva-ghāta or pañca-mahābhūta (GjPt; cf. Padfield 1986: 200). There are ten such airs; it is the dhanañjaya prāṇa or vāyu which remains in the skull and will create a ghost unless released (UPBrM; GjVF). According to a Puṣṭimārgī swami:

> We pray to dhanañjay prān, 'Please you go out from the body.' We believe that the ātmā lives for ten days at the place of dying, so we burn a candle at that place, and that candle continues for ten days. The ātmā does not reside in the body [but remains at the home where the person has died]. The remaining nine prāṇas merge in the pañca-mahābhūtas. (Gj32)

However, many of Parry's informants defined death

> as the instant at which the prāṇ or 'vital breath' leaves the body...This occurs—not at the cessation of physiological functioning—but at the rite of kapāla kriyā, which is performed mid-way through the cremation,

before which it is 'commonly said to be completely inappropriate to use the term *preta* "a disembodied ghost"'. The implication of this is that the corpse is, in some sense, animate.

> As another informant spontaneously put it, 'He does not die but is killed. He dies on the pyre.' (Parry 1982: 79f)

Parry goes on to suggest that the cremation is thus a sacrifice, in which the chief mourner becomes a homicide, and the subsequent purifications are performed in accordance with this (cf. Evison 1989: 53ff). Regarding the body as a sacrifice would, of course, mean that it would have to be circumambulated clockwise, in the auspicious direction. Although my own informants, including four in Varanasi, did not regard the cremation as a true sacrifice (despite the implications of the term *antyeṣṭi* 'final sacrifice'), it seems that there is a process taking place, either through the kapāla-kriyā or the pot-breaking, by which the ātman becomes disconnected at some level from the remaining prāṇa in the skull, so that it 'receives a message' and 'knows that it is dead' (VrPt42). In either view the implications in Britain of not performing a cremation for a week or more are extremely grave for the ātman.

A brahmin informant at the burning ghat in Varanasi said the chief mourner did not always break the skull. When the body was nearly burned, most people returned home and 'three or four stone-hearted people' remained to 'break the head with a stick from the stretcher'. He said that the kapāla-kriyā was very difficult to watch and very traumatic for the people doing it—some men pass out—so that in the Panjab and Uttar Pradesh the chief mourner does not have to stay. In Varanasi the chief mourner can buy a pot from Dom Raj, the head of the Dom community (p. 68), and break it instead of the skull; as he leaves he places Ganges water, rice, sesame and money in the pot, puts it on his right shoulder and breaks it by throwing it backwards, and then walks away without looking back.

The pot-breaking ceremony, with its variations, seems to be common in most parts of India (cf. Evison 1989: 52ff). It takes place, as has been seen, at one of three stages—at the entrance to the cremation ground, after the pradakṣiṇās but before the body is cremated, or after the cremation, sometimes (as above) as a substitute for the breaking of the skull (Evison 1989: 56ff). In addition to this specific function, it seems to have the function of breaking the bond between the deceased and the chief mourner, who

> must not do anything which might re-establish the links with the world of the dead which have been so carefully broken in this ritual: to have any further contact with the corpse would encourage death and the denizens of the funeral ground to follow the relatives back to the village (Evison 1989: 56).[10]

Should the death occur during five inauspicious days each lunar month (pañcaka: the last five of the twenty-seven lunar mansions), then drastic action has to be taken, especially if the person is young; otherwise more people will die within five days. Evison suggests that this time is dangerous beause

> as the moon wanes the distinction between the world of the living and that of the dead becomes blurred and the barriers which separate the two realms are at their weakest. If a person dies during this time the force of death cannot be repelled and claims other victims before a proper distinction between the two worlds is restored as the moon waxes. In the case of death under an inauspicious asterism the family do not fear the deceased's ghost so much as death itself, acting as an impersonal force (1989: 169ff; cf. *GP* 2, 4, 176ff; 35, 17ff).

According to some informants, it is cremation during this time which is more dangerous than the actual death. If the cremation cannot be delayed, then the family have to make five effigies of barley flour (PjBr) or darbha grass (Delhi Br) and cremate them with the dead, in a special ritual called pañcaka-śānti. Otherwise four or five more people will die, or as many as there are days left in pañcaka (*GP* 2, 4, 181-2).

The return in India

The women will only have gone part of the way on the journey to the cremation ground, to the edge of the village or to the crossroads, where they may place a dīvā, and then return to the house which they sweep and clean. The bed the deceased slept on should be thrown out

10 Parry sees the pot as symbolizing both the womb and the body. The last thing the mahābrāhmaṇa does as he walks away on the eleventh day after conducting the śrāddha is to break a pot (personal communication).

'because of disease, but now because of cost people do not do it' (GjPlF56). After cleaning the house the women bathe. Some Gujaratis place red powder or flour on the floor where the body lay, and place a basket over it, before the procession leaves; and when the male mourners return, it is raised to see what pattern there is underneath, as this will indicate the kind of rebirth the ātman has taken (somewhat at variance with the view that it will take ten to twelve days for the preta to form a new body). Informants claim to have seen the figure of a man, of Kṛṣṇa, of *oṃ*, and of a snake. In some families the widow's bangles are broken on the body; in others, after it has left the house:

> This is the sign the husband is leaving, so when the body has been taken the ladies will be collected and the one who has become a widow will be sitting in the centre, and her bangles will be broken by a stone, and it is very pitiable...They all make her aware that 'now you are a widow'. (GjPlF60)

The returning men will wash or bathe at the cremation ground and wash at home—'The women provide the water and pour it without touching' (PjBrM42)—and 'pay respect to God with a [lighted] incense stick and each person will take dhūpa, passing their hands [over the smoke and then] over their face and neck', for purification. A new fire will be prepared in the courtyard and people will walk round it before going inside (PjKhM62).

No food will have been eaten between the death and the cremation, unless there is an abnormal delay. Women are allowed to cook in some households, but to help them, friends and relatives come with their own food; in other households food is not cooked in the house but will be supplied by the in-laws of the son of the deceased, who are not affected by sūtaka, on the first, fourth, eleventh and thirteenth days.

Stage III: Preparation of the body in Britain

In Britain, the nature and sequence of events has undergone a transformation. Much of the decision-making and control from the moment of death, especially relating to the disposal of the body, has been taken out of the hands of the family—because of the bureaucracy surrounding death, the need for a post-mortem in some instances, for a funeral director, and for a coffin. The body will have been removed from the home or hospital at death and kept in an undertaker's until the day of the cremation. Timing depends entirely on other people. The one advantage of a delay between the death and the funeral is that relatives from overseas can get here. However, immigration law may prevent this, which can cause extreme distress.

In the early days of the community the body was sometimes prepared shortly after death in the mortuary, but this was so unpleasant that it may be one reason why the custom was changed:

> It was a terrifying experience and it was just one room and there was

> another dead body there which was just opened and all they had there was just a screen. Every time I was going around [to dress my brother] I was looking at two bodies...My uncle helped me a lot and I had to do it because the other people who should have offered didn't because they were scared. (GjDjM35)

A second reason why the custom changed was the need to present the body for agni saṃskāra (cremation) in a state of purity, so it would be necessary to bathe the body immediately beforehand. The chief mourner with his male relatives or caste peers will prepare the body of a male relative; women prepare the body of a woman. Young women are not allowed to participate, so older female relatives or caste peers will go, and there is a former nurse in the community who sometimes assists. The eldest son is expected to participate in the preparation of his father's body, which can be quite traumatic if he is young and unaccustomed to the sight of a corpse; in any case, the bathing of a body a week or ten days after the death creates obvious problems. The funeral directors most commonly used have cooperated with the families to meet their needs in this respect; one informant observed that they were more sympathetic than the doctors. There are caste traditions as to how the body should be washed—some use water, either washing fully or sprinkling, while others use yoghurt or milk, and it is a great help if there is a senior member of the family to give guidance. In one family the father died suddenly from a heart attack. An uncle who was visiting from India was able to give guidance; and he, another uncle and the three sons prepared the body, which was 'quite terrifying, quite traumatic...We were just chanting religious things at the same time, trying to keep my mind off it' (PjKhM). The body is dressed in the sort of clothes normally worn, new if possible, including socks and shoes, so there is a shift from the ideal of a dhoti or loose covering. A woman, as in India, will be dressed in a white sari if widowed, and her wedding sari if predeceasing her husband. The body is placed back in the coffin, and often covered with a beautiful shawl or cloth. It is then taken to the family home in a hearse, where the first part of the funeral will be held.

The funeral in Britain: The domestic ceremony

Many of the rituals which are performed in the house here during the domestic part of the funeral are adaptations either of domestic rituals which would have been performed immediately after death in relation to the body, such as its orientation and the circumambulations (Stage III), or of rituals which, in India, would be performed at the cremation ground (Stage V), but which would be impossible in the crematorium, for reasons of both design and time. The ritual journey (Stage IV) is reduced to a drive in the hearse from the undertaker's, where the body will have been prepared, to the house for part of the funeral, and then to the crematorium for the remainder, without stops along the way (cf. p. 4). If piṇḍas are offered, they are offered in the home and usually placed in the coffin. Thus Stages III to V, which in India normally form a continuum with Stage II (death) within twenty-four hours, are separated from it by as much as a week; and Stage IV (the ritual journey) has virtually disappeared.

To an observer, the ceremony at home seems to be the most significant part of the funeral, not least because the whole family is present, including women and often children. There is rather more time than is permitted at the crematorium, and there is more freedom to perform whatever rituals are possible in the circumstances (pp. 76f). Because it is normally possible to display the body, it is possible to place various substances on it which in India would have been placed on it prior to the cremation journey or at the cremation ground.

Several informants have spoken of funerals conducted without a pandit (pp. 54f). All those I observed had a pandit conducting them, with considerable variety in the ways this was done. For convenience, the ceremony in the home will be described as the funeral, which is how it tends to be referred to, perhaps reflecting the changing pattern of events; the ceremony at the crematorium will be referred to as the cremation. In either situation there may be a eulogy.

One pandit sends a list of what he will need to the family in advance, advising them what materials should be prepared, and stresses that the house should be quiet and orderly, because sometimes he has found havoc. He tries to arrive at least half an hour early to start the prayers and mantras, and if it can be arranged, suggests the family gather for a private ritual before the body arrives from the undertaker's. Thālīs (circular trays) are prepared with all the necessary ingredients: piṇḍas. tulsi leaves, flowers, Ganges water, various powders, incense sticks, sandalwood, yoghurt, and sesame seeds. Ārya Samājīs and many other Panjabis also have havan sāmagrī (herbs for the sacred fire). A small bit of gold is needed, which may be taken from the wife's maṅgala-sūtra (marriage necklace) if she has just been widowed, but some priests do not like to do this and prefer new gold, which the Indian goldsmith will always give for no charge. The furniture will have been removed from the living-room, and white cloths spread on the floor (p. 79), sometimes sprinkled with pañca-gavya and Ganges water; and flowers, rice and kumkum (red powder) may be placed on it.

The body will arrive by hearse from the undertaker's in its 'box'—a disparaging term, as the coffin is disliked—and is brought into the house by male relatives and friends who 'give shoulder' to it as a sacred obligation. If the house is very small it may have to be brought in through the window, or turned on end to negotiate the front passage, which may shift the body, to the distress of the family. It should be brought in feet first, since people enter the house feet first, and then placed on trestles in the living-room, which is packed with family, friends, and community members. The body is oriented as it would have been in India at the time of death (cf. p. 60). As with the pandits in India, there is some disagreement as to the correct direction. A Gujarati pandit carries a compass to ensure the head is to the north; a Bihari pandit insists it should be to the south.

At all the funerals I have observed in Britain, the mourners stood as the coffin was brought in, and began chanting the Gāyatrī mantra, although, according to the pandits, no Vedic mantras should be chanted during sūtaka (Stevenson 1920: 164). Other phrases which may be chanted include 'rādhe kṛṣṇa, gopāla kṛṣṇa', 'śrī kṛṣṇaḥ śaraṇaṃ mama', 'oṃ namaḥ śivāya', 'oṃ namo bhagavate vāsudevāya' ('Homage to Lord Kṛṣṇa'), and 'śrī rāma jaya rāma, jaya jaya rāma' ('Victory to Rāma').

The coffin is opened, with the family standing on the right side of the body and the pandit on the left. The sons and the rest of the immediate family are called upon to perform ācamana (sipping water) and then touching themselves from head to neck, neck to waist, and waist to feet, as a purification. This symbolizes the three lokas: heaven, earth, and below the earth. Then saṃkalpa is performed, which is a declaration of intent, explaining what is to be done and for whom:

> This is my prayer for the departed soul that I am offering. May this soul have sadgati, the happy ending. 'O my father or mother, you were here all these days with us. Now you have left the body. May I offer my prayer to see that your soul journey will be happy, and I, as a son, will perform my duty to see you have a safe journey. (KanPt)

The chief mourner then moves the sacred thread from the left shoulder (the auspicious side) to the right (the inauspicious side). If he has no thread, one is made on the spot from white cotton. The chief mourner or priest may chant eight stanzas of the *Gaṅgā Stotra* or the *Puruṣa Sūkta (ṚV* 10, 90), and then the chief mourner places Ganges water in the mouth of the deceased, with tulsi, gold, yoghurt, ghi or pañcāmṛta (p. 64), although one Bihari pandit felt the last was not really śāstrika, and was only appropriate for bathing a deity. Other members of the family follow suit if there is time, and put a tilak of sandalwood paste on the forehead of a married woman, or sidhur (a red paste) in her parting. Rice, sesame and darbha grass may be put on top of the body; pink and white powders are also sprinkled on, and flowers or petals will be scattered over it. The family should do this, but if time is short they will touch the chief mourner as he does it. The body may be garlanded. Four or five coconuts should be given by the sons, one for each direction (although at one Ārya Samājī funeral only pieces of coconut were placed on the body), and the widow may, either now or later, place one on the chest.

When the body has thus been decorated, six piṇḍas should be offered (cf. p. 66), although at almost all the funerals I attended only one was offered, if at all. Most of the pandits interviewed said they insisted on six, and often had to argue their case with the older members of the community, explaining the piṇḍas were necessary to protect both ātman and body against bhūts (evil spirits) (cf. p. 66). According to a Gujarati pandit, three piṇḍas should be placed on the right and three on the left, near the hands. Various other items may be placed in the coffin: a kuntī (rosary), sandalwood, agarbatti (incense sticks), and ghi, which may be applied to the soles of the feet and the palms of the hands, or applied all over. Some communities just put in packets of butter. Havan sāmagrī may also be sprinkled on the body.

The family now do four pradakṣiṇās (or five if the wife is still living), the widow in front carrying a coconut in both hands, unless the eldest son is there to lead the family. The Bihari pandit said that in India the wife normally does nothing, and only does this in Britain for consolation. Sometimes the mourners want to take lighted incense sticks around the body and touch them to the lips of the corpse (mukhāgni), because they cannot light the pyre at the cremation ground. However, the pandits discourage this as inappropriate in the house, because it is not the cremation, although pushing the coffin into the furnace (p. 77) is not really a substitute: 'We are living in a culture where we are not in control' (BihPt65). Those who do this touch the right toe and sometimes the head and sides as a symbol of lighting the fire, then go round four times and place the sticks in the coffin. Some communities use a clay pot, containing incense and rice and other substances, to circumambulate the corpse, but this was never observed. However, at the funeral of an elderly Panjabi woman the eldest son carried a pot of water round the coffin and broke it just outside the front door, on instruction from the pandit, as the coffin was removed from the house, although at a later interview he did not remember doing so.

As the family goes round, starting from the feet, they take sesame, flowers and other substances, and on the fourth round, bow low and touch the feet of the corpse. Finally, after the outsiders have paid their respects, the eldest or youngest son will go round again, chanting God's name. If his father has died, he bows low, crying, 'Bābūjī, Bābūjī', which, according to the pandits, is lokācāra (a local tradition), not a rule (cf. p. 63). The priest, meanwhile, may be reading a passage such as chapter 2, 8 or 15 of the *BhG*, or the 'Thousand names of Viṣṇu'. A cloth (kafan), which is usually white, although for brahmins it can be a richly coloured silk, is placed on the body; if the deceased is a married woman, her family will provide this. Then, if a husband has died, the widow is brought to the coffin to say goodbye, and this may be the stage at which she will take off her coloured bangles and place them in the coffin, although some communities force them off or break them for her, which the pandits find very distressing: 'The widows want to bring her into their own camp' (BihPt). The lid is closed, and the mourners chant something such as 'oṃ namo bhagavate vāsudevāya'. As the coffin leaves there may be unrestrained weeping by the women; while the men are more restrained, emotion shown by sons or very close relatives does not seem to be frowned on (see pp. 67, 79).

Swāminārāyaṇ informants do not think a pandit is necessary except for the śrāddha. Pramukh Swāmī, the leader of the Akshar Purushottam Samsthā branch of the movement, had told a Patel family that 'the only ceremony of concern was the coconut, doing ārtī and saying goodbye to the body'. The son described his father's funeral, at which the principal features were the reading of the *BhG*, as 'God's message that the person has not really died but has gone to his place, to heaven'; and a water-offering to make sure 'the soul goes to heaven or rests in peace, so that it doesn't come back to earth because he didn't get food or water' (cf. p. 62). Finally the eldest son made a vow to fast for two months, on the eleventh day, 'so that whatever sins he had done got washed away'.

Stage V: The cremation in Britain

The journey to the crematorium takes place in a hearse, with the family in a limousine; there are no stops on the way. In all the funerals I have attended in Southampton, the mourners have followed in double-decker buses. Panjabi women have attended cremations in their own community, but Gujarati women do not go.

The crematorium officials like the mourners to go in first, with the coffin following; but this has created arguments sometimes, since the Indian tradition is to follow the body (cf. Stevenson 1920: 148). There are a few prayers and mantras, and the *BhG* may be read, although this is regarded as quite inappropriate at the cremation by some pandits. A short eulogy may be made, although a Gujarati pandit was told in no uncertain terms at one funeral that the mourners did not want a lecture. After the prayers the chief mourner presses the button for the coffin to disappear, and then goes down below to ignite the cremator or to push the coffin in, an experience which some find very traumatic. Meanwhile a Śiva shrine may be set up outside, with a pile of rice, a dīvā and agarbattī. The sons and then the other mourners do a short pūjā, offering money before returning home.[11] Here they will sprinkle themselves with water before entering the house, although Gujaratis of the strict Swāmīnārāyaṇ and Puṣṭimārga sects will bathe and change in a friend's house before returning home. For a time everyone returns to the house and sits quietly on the sheet-covered floor, before returning to their own homes, except for the relatives. Friends and neighbours bring in simple, spice-free food to feed the visiting relatives, of whom there may be a great number, from various parts of the United Kingdom, India, East Africa and the United States.

In some Panjabi families the pandit will return for a havan immediately after the funeral. This seems to be a modified Ārya Samājī tradition, and informants said that in East Africa the Ārya Samājīs completed all the ceremonies by the fourth day, when traditionally the ashes are collected, because Swāmī Dayānanda Saraswatī did not believe in sūtaka, or in the conventional śrāddha ceremonies (Dayānanda 1975: 337; 419-23). Following the havan, the eldest son (and in some families all the sons) is presented with a turban (pagṛī) by his

11 There is quite strong disagreement among pandits in Britain as to whether people do, or should, worship at a Śiva shrine after a cremation. A number of informants say it is customary, particularly as Śiva is lord of the cremation ground, and I have observed it on several occasions. However, several pandits said emphatically that no worship at a Śiva shrine should take place during sutaka.

wife's family, as a sign that he is now responsible for younger members of the family, unmarried sisters, and his mother. The pandit at one such ceremony gave a little talk to the eldest son, telling him that he was now the head of the household and should take his responsibilities seriously and not provoke his younger brothers, while they were in turn told to obey and respect him. They all then presented their mother with gold bangles and saris as a sign that they would care for her. This completes the ceremonies, although another havan may be offered on the twelfth day, with gifts to the brahmins (p. 80). The local pandit feels it is mistaken to perform havan during sūtaka, since Vedic mantras should not be chanted during this period. When he refused to do this for a recent funeral, the family invited a priest from London instead.

Stage VI: Disposing of the ashes

While there is a great contrast between the procedures and the timing of the gathering of the bones and ashes in India and Britain, there may be little difference in their disposal, especially if members of the family travel to India, or even post them, so that they can be deposited in the Ganges. In India, the bones and ashes are usually collected on the third day; the term used is *phūl chānnā* 'picking flowers' (cf. *GP* 2, 5, 15). The ashes are separated from the bones and thrown into the nearest river. The bones are washed, and kept until they can be taken to a sacred river. If it can be afforded, the ideal is to divide the bones into three parts and take them to Allahabad, Varanasi and Hardwar. In Britain, the gathering of the ashes is not attended with any rituals since they are already packaged by the crematorium. If they are to be disposed of locally, the local pandit may accompany the chief mourner to the river or sea and then proceed with the śrāddhā; otherwise the ashes will be posted or taken to India when convenient (but before an eclipse), and the śrāddhā is arranged at the usual time (cf. Poulter 1986: 234f).

Sūtaka

In India, the time from the cremation to at least the tenth day is marked by extreme sūtaka, simple food and an ascetic lifestyle. Men do not shave, the family sleep on the floor, and sexual intercourse, sweet food, music and social activities are avoided; food and drink are not offered to guests. There is no worship of the gods or goddesses; they are removed to another house, or covered. A lamp is kept burning in the house at the place of death, and if it goes out it is a bad sign requiring remedial action. Another lamp may be kept burning in a pipal tree near the burning ground, next to a pot of water with a tiny hole, for the purpose of nourishing the ghost, until the tenth-day ceremonies. From the third day onwards, the *GP* may be recited (Stevenson 1920: 155), although many Hindus prefer the *BhG*. People visit throughout this time to pay their respects; as has been mentioned (p. 67), the women are expected to weep freely, while the men, who talk together in small groups, show more restraint.

Whereas in India it might be said that the 'mourning proper' begins after the mourners return home from the cremation, British Hindus observe sūtaka as far as possible for eight or ten days *before* the cremation. While the rules may be understood, it is not always possible for mourners to stay away from work for the full mourning period, so it is not thought practical for men to remain unshaven throughout sūtaka. Many of the stricter families, however, still observe the prohibitions, and the men may be unshaven until the śrāddha on the tenth day, especially if they do not have to go to work. (They do not, to my knowledge, have their heads shaved for the cremation (cf. p. 65).) Friends will help with food preparation at the outset, but often families resume cooking because it is not convenient to depend on others for such a long time (cf. p. 72). Furniture is removed and white sheets are spread on the floor (p. 74). Visitors stream in to pay their condolences, and periods of quiet weeping by the women may be interspersed by readings and talking. As in India, the *GP* or *BhG* may be read; East African Panjabis may gather to read a long poem, the *Amṛta Varṣa*. Generally there is more restraint than in India.

The texts, with some variations, prescribe ten days of sūtaka for brahmins, twelve for kṣatriyas, fifteen for vaiśyas and a month for śūdras (*Manu* 5, 83; Kane 1953: 271; Tambiah 1973), so that the sapiṇḍī-karaṇa (below) is held for non-brahmins during the period of sūtaka (cf. p. 78). The differentiation by varṇa is reflected to some extent in current practice; for instance, many brahmins end sūtaka on the tenth day, and business castes such as Vanyas, Lohānas and some Khatris end it on the sixteenth or seventeenth day. But Patels, who are also a business caste, end it on the twelfth or thirteenth day, while some Kumhārs (potters) claiming kṣatriya status end it on the sixteenth day, and so do some Panjabi brahmins.

Stages VII-IX: śrāddhas; end of sūtaka

Śrāddhas are rituals in which piṇḍas are offered for the nourishment of the deceased ancestors of the family, either collectively at fixed times of the year (pārvana-śrāddha), or for a particular deceased person at times reckoned from the day of death (ekoddiṣṭa-śrāddha).

During the ten days after death, the preta is nourished by regular tarpaṇa (offerings of water), and food, which should include a piṇḍa each day to create a new body for it; but ten piṇḍas are often offered on the tenth day instead (Stevenson 1920: 159).

As well as on the tenth day, according to the texts, śrāddhas are performed on the eleventh and twelfth days after death, to enable the deceased to move on to his or her next life. (If death was violent or unnatural, there may be a nārāyaṇa bali on the eleventh day.) These culminate in the sapiṇḍī-karaṇa, on the twelfth or thirteenth[12] day,

12 The day chosen depends on the relative auspiciousness of the days of the week. Sunday, Tuesday and Wednesday are avoided.

which enables the preta to become an ancestor (pitṛ). Even in India these are often condensed into one; in Britain they are usually on the twelfth or thirteenth day. The local temple pandit, or a visiting one, may attend; if the ashes are to be taken to a river or the sea, he may accompany them. In some instances a close male relative has been asked to arrange the ritual in India on behalf of the family.

At the end of sūtaka the house will be cleaned, and purified by sprinkling with milk and water; in India this would be done with cow-dung or pañca-gavya. The clothes of the deceased may be given to Oxfam. The end of sūtaka is marked by a feast to which brahmins are invited, and brahmins are given clothes, money and food. Another feast for brahmins and family members may be held at the end of a month; at a recent one, bhajans were sung in the temple, a meal provided for several hundred people, and steel thālīs, engraved with the name and dates of the deceased, given to everyone present. There may be further feasts and gifts three, six or twelve months after death, corresponding to the śrāddhas which take place at these times in India, although the piṇḍa offerings which may be made in India are not normally made in Britain, and the procedures are greatly simplified. The ending of sūtaka, and the reduction in the mourning restrictions on the immediate family, may take place gradually over a year, which according to some informants is the time taken by the soul to become a pitṛ or reach its destination.

There is an annual śrāddha during pitṛ pakṣa, the lunar fortnight around October when known ancestors are honoured on the lunar day equivalent to that of their death. There is another on the tithi, the anniversary of the day of death by the lunar calendar. Most Hindus interviewed in Southampton held that the important śrāddha is during the pitṛ pakṣa; however, the temple recently instituted a scheme whereby members can pay £201 to have a tithi each year on the anniversary of the death, reckoned by the Gregorian calendar because of the difficulty of booking dates in advance by the Hindu calendar. On both occasions the pandit may recite some mantras on behalf of the deceased, gifts are made to the pandit or to the poor, and brahmins are invited to a meal. On the tithi, the community is invited to share a meal in the temple.

Conclusion

While many Hindus experience some anxiety about the appropriate performance of death rituals, others are pragmatic about what is possible, believing that as long as they have done their best, there will be no negative results. The continued contacts with India provide considerable reassurance here, since many families still have relatives there who can arrange ceremonies on their behalf, the most important being the śrāddha ceremonies on the tenth to twelfth days. The biggest problem seems to centre on the death itself: the failure to be with someone at death is a disaster for any community, but for Hindus there are long-term repercussions both for the ātman and for the survivors (cf. p. 63). As has been seen, this also creates problems for hospitals unless there are facilities for enabling the patient to be in a room alone with his family, with minimum disruption for other patients. This needs a high level of understanding, both at the administrative level and on the part of doctors and nurses caring for the patients.[13]

For the pandits, there is a continuous process of trying to adapt to changed circumstances, knowing that they are having to compromise, both in terms of their own training and orientation and in terms of time. Many of them feel the funeral rituals are not their job, possibly because of the pollution, and because of the stigma attached to the performance of funeral rituals in India and to the receipt of the gifts associated with them. A Gujarati pandit, the son of a temple priest, was told he should not perform funerals; but he had come to Britain to pray for God's grace for his sick wife and had received it, so he felt obliged to serve. Some Puṣṭimārgīs had argued with him because they said this would make him impure, to which he had retorted, 'How many of you came here without bathing?' They made the lame excuse that they had not gone into the inner temple, but he said he would go to help at a time of need, and afterwards bathe and change, and after tārā snāna ('star bath', when the stars appear), he would be pure enough to perform pūjā.

For many pandits, the receipt of gifts is a problem, because they feel called upon to receive things for a funeral which in India would only be given to the mahābrāhmaṇas. The priest is standing as surrogate for the deceased, so that by receiving the gift he is taking on the burden of the sin of the departed person. Some refuse; others take the gifts because it is essential for the well-being of the soul and the mourners, but they do extra penances and prayers to deal with the burden. The above-mentioned Gujarati pandit will often pray all night in preparation. Another pandit said, 'The dān has to be proper, not just 50p. If we don't like [it], then we can give it to the temple' (GjPt70), and all the pandits said they gave gifts away again, sometimes just retaining basic expenses.

A Gujarati pandit admitted that he did not always understand the mantras but still had to pray. 'I feel guilty because I must understand what I utter; because people will take my word for granted as good and correct.' Another learned pandit said that the priests have a big responsibility to ensure clients do the proper ritual so that the deceased goes to the proper place:

> If I pose with knowledge which I don't have it is a sin; I don't know, [but] I have posed as if I [do] know. I have led you in the wrong way and the poor chap won't get sadgati, a good end...If a son is doing an incorrect ritual with all devotion, thinking it is a death ritual, the spirit, if it has

13 There is a gradual change taking place, with courses and seminars for social workers and medical staff on multicultural aspects of death and bereavement. The Open University is producing a new half-credit course, Death and Dying (K699), in 1992; I am writing two articles on the subject for the Reader for this course.

> knowledge, will suffer because it is not the right mantra. If I want to go to Oxford Circus you mustn't put me in a bus for Southall. If we don't perform the proper ceremonies what will happen to us? (KanPt)

Another pandit said that if it was not done properly it would rise up in the unconscious all the time. The constraints of time mean that only the minimum of rituals can be done, and the saṃkalpa, vidhis (prescribed ritual acts) and pindas are having to be done at home instead of at the cremation. It is not possible to pay as much attention to astrological charts as in India; however, one pandit said that it was still essential to perform a special addition to the funeral during pañcaka (p. 71), but he quietly took the five effigies with him, only discussing it with the chief mourner or senior relatives to avoid causing pain and anxiety.

Several pandits feel that there is a need to have a standardized service for Britain. One has been produced by the National Council for Hindu Temples (1987), but they are critical of it because of its use of the *BhG*, which is

> not for the soul. It is for the comfort of the mourners, but this isn't a proper funeral prayer.

The funeral prayer should be directed towards two things: one for the elements making up the body (the pañca-tattva), the other for the elements making up the spiritual body (the prāṇa-tattva). The correct rituals should be obtained by a suitably learned priest from a karmakāṇḍa.

> The ślokas from the *Gītā* about casting off our clothes [*BhG* 2, 22] is for our knowledge, but God, Agni, Yama will not accept that as a prayer. It is all right to read the *Gītā* at home, but it is not appropriate at the cremation. (GjPt65)

It can be seen that there is a shift in both the pattern and emphasis of the funeral rituals. The cremation journey with its halts, the offering of piṇḍas, and the breaking of the pot, have either disappeared or lost their emphasis; the cremation itself has altered radically, with no open pyre, no circumambulations at the crematorium, and no kapāla-kriyā. The fire can only be offered indirectly, and many of the last rites are performed in the home instead, with the pandit in attendance when possible. For some Hindus this has become the focal point of the funeral, and is especially important for Gujarati women who cannot go to the crematorium (p. 67). Despite the efforts of the pandits, the purpose of the service at the crematorium may be shifting towards the consolation of the mourners in this world, rather than being concerned solely with the welfare of the dead in the unseen world, although this may not be recognized. In due course, as some of the rituals disappear or alter, such as the pot-breaking and the kapāla-kriyā, the beliefs that go with them may also change. The pandits are working out an adapted form of ritual which is appropriate to the circumstances, but whether there is eventually a standardized form, or a variety of forms as at present, remains to be seen.

Nevertheless, much has been retained, and provides great strength in the community, with tremendous support and cohesion at the time of a death. Although the concept of the good death can only be understood, in Hindu society, in the context of its opposite, bad death, it nevertheless provides a useful model of a philosophical approach to death; and a study of Hindu belief and practice is of value at a time when there is a growing awareness among professionals in Britain of the need to help people to die with dignity and to legitimate the need for adequate mourning.[14]

14 To be dealt with more fully in my thesis, in progress at the time of writing.

[Overleaf: Chart of the timing of death rituals in India and Britain.]

The timing of death rituals in India and in Britain

Timing	Stage in India	Period of sūtaka:	Stage in Britain
	I: Preparation for death		I: Preparation for death
Day 1	II: Death III: Preparation of body IV: Piṇḍa-dāna and journey to cremation ground V: Cremation		II: Death; removal of body to undertakers'
Day 2			
Day 3	VI: Collection of bones (ĀS: end of rituals; end of śoka, with havan and pagṛī)		
Day 4			VIII: Some relatives may have to return to work
Day 5			
Day 6			
Day 7			III: Preparation of body at undertakers' IV: Domestic stage of funeral
Day 8			V: Cremation (ĀS: end of śoka, with havan and pagṛī)
Day 9			VI: Ashes received from crematorium
Day 10	VII: Ashes to river; śrāddha (10 piṇḍas)	Brahmin	
Day 11	VII: śrāddha		
Day 12	VII: Sapiṇḍī-karaṇa; gifts to brahmins; feast	Patel	VII: Sapiṇḍī-karaṇa (may be done in India). Ashes to river or sea; feast
Day 13	VIII: Gifts to brahmins		VIII: Feast; gifts to brahmins
Day 16	VIII: End of śoka for most communities; feast	Lohāna	VIII: End of śoka for most communities; feast
	IX: Annual śrāddhas		IX: Annual śrāddhas

Continuous lines indicate the period over which a stage normally extends.

Broken lines indicate the period over which a stage or group of stages may extend, or within which it may occur.

ABBREVIATIONS AND REFERENCES

In references to informants, figures indicate the approximate age of the informant. E.g., PjBrF40 indicates a Panjabi brahmin woman aged about forty.

AGS: *Āśvalāyana Gṛhya Sūtra.*
All ER: *All England Law Reports.*
AIR: *All India Reporter.*
AS: Ārya Samāj.
AV: *Atharva-Veda.*
BhG: *Bhagavad-Gītā.*
Bih: Bihar.
Br: brahmin.
BṛhUp: *Bṛhad-Āranyaka Upaniṣad.*
ChUp: *Chāndogya Upaniṣad.*
Dj: Darji.
DhT: *Dharma-tattva.*
F: female.
Gj: Gujarati.
GP: *Garuḍa Purāṇa.*
H: Hindi.
HMA: *Hindu Marriage Act* 1955.
ĪśUp: *Īsā Upaniṣad.*
Kan: Kannada.
KGS: *Kauśika Gṛhya Sūtra.*
Kh: Khatri.
M: male.
Mah: Maharashtrian.
Manu: *Manu-smṛti.*
MBh: *Mahābhārata.*
MS: *Maitrāyaṇi Saṃhitā.*
OED: *Oxford English Dictionary.*
Pj: Panjabi.
Pl: Patel.
Pt: pandit.
Pu: purohita.
ṚV: *Ṛg-Veda.*
ŚBr: *Śatapatha Brāhmaṇa.*
SkP: *Skanda Purāṇa.*
Skt: Sanskrit.
TBr: *Taittirīya Brāhmaṇa.*
TS: *Taittirīya Saṃhitā.*
UP: Uttar Pradesh.
V: Vanya.
VajUp: *Vajrasūcī Upaniṣad.*
Vr: Varanasi.
VS: *Vedānta-Sūtra.*

Antoine, R. (1953). 'A pioneer of neo-Hinduism'. *Indica*. Bombay, Indian Historical Research Institute. 5-21.

Babb, L.A. (1975). *The Divine Hierarchy*. New York: Columbia University Press.

Banerjea, Krishna Mohan (1851). 'Hindu caste'. *Calcutta Review 15*. 36-75.

Basham, A. L. (1967). *The Wonder that was India*. London: Fontana.

Bose, Nirmal Kumar (1959). 'Some aspects of caste in Bengal'. *Traditional India: Structure and Change*, ed. Milton Singer. Philadelphia: American Folklore Society. 191-206.

Brockington, J. L. (1981). *The Sacred Thread: Hinduism in Its Continuity and Diverstiy*. Edinburgh: Edinburgh University Press.

Bühler, G. (1886). *The Laws of Manu: Translated with extracts from seven commentaries*. Oxford: Clarendon Press. Reprinted Delhi: Motilal Banarsidass, 1975.

Burghart, R. (ed.) (1987). *Hinduism in Great Britain. The Perpetuation of Religion in an Alien Cultural Milieu*. London: Tavistock.

Clarke, Colin, Peach, Ceri and Vertovec, Steven (eds.) (1990). *South Asians Overseas: Migration and Ethnicity*. Cambridge: Cambridge University Press.

Chatterji, Bankim Chandra (1969): *Baṅkim Racanābalī* (collected works of Bankim Chandra Chatterji). 3 vols. Calcutta: Sāhitya Saṃsad. References are to vol. II.

Colebrooke, H. T. (1798). 'Enumeration of Indian classes'. *Asiatic Researches 5*. 53-67. Reprinted in his *Essays on the Religion and Philosophy of the Hindus*. London: Williams & Norgate 1837; 2nd edn 1858. 270-279.

Collet, S. D. (1962). *The life and letters of Raja Rammohun Roy*, 3rd edn. Calcutta: Sadharan Brahmo Samaj.

Cormack, Margaret (1961). *The Hindu Woman*. Bombay: Asia Publishing House.

CRE (1990). *Britain: A Plural Society. Report of a Seminar by the Commission for Racial Equality and the Runnymede Trust*. London: Commission for Racial Equality.

Crooke, W. (1917). 'Out-castes (Indian)'. *Encyclopaedia of Religions and Ethics, vol. 9,*

ed. J. Hastings, Edinburgh: T. & T. Clarke, 581f.
Das, Veena (1970). 'The uses of liminality: society and cosmos in Hinduism'. *Contributions to Indian Sociology (NS) 10* 245-63.
Das, Veena (1977). *Structure and Cognition: Aspects of Hindu Caste and Ritual.* Delhi: Oxford University Press.
Das, Veena (1985). 'Paradigms of body symbolism: an analysis of selected themes in Hindu culture'. *Indian Religion,* ed. R. Burghart and A. Cantlie. London: Curzon. 180-207.
Dayānanda Sarasvatī (1975). *Light of Truth.* Delhi: Sarvadeshik Arya Pratinidhi Sabha. (Tr. of the following.)
Dayānanda Sarasvatī (1972a). *Satyārtha Prakāśa.* Bahalgarh: Ramlal Kapur Trust.
Dayānanda Sarasvatī (1972b). *The Light of Truth,* tr. Durga Prasad, 3rd edn. Delhi: Jan Gyan Prakashan. (Tr of the above.)
De, Sushil Kumar (1962). *Bengali Literature in the Nineteenth Century.* Calcutta: Firma K. L. Mukhopadhyay.
Deb, Rādhākānta (1967). *Śabda-kalpadruma,* reprint, 5 vols. Varanasi: Chowkhamba (first published 1815-58).
Derrett, J. D. M. (1968). 'Hindu: a definition wanted for the purpose of applying a personal law'. *Zeitschrift für vergleichende Rechtswissenschaft 70.* 110-28.
Derrett, J. D. M. (1970). *A Critique of Modern Hindu Law.* Bombay: N. M. Tripathi.
Derrett, J. D. M. (1976). 'The discussion of marriage by Gadādhara'. J. D. M. Derrett, *Essays in Classical and Modern Hindu Law, vol. I.* Leiden: Brill. 303-32.
Diehl, C. G. (1956). *Instrument and Purpose in South Indian Religion.* Lund: Håkon Ohlsson.
Diwan, Paras (1982). *Modern Hindu Law.* 5th edn reprint. Allahabad: Allahabad Law Agency.
Dubois, Abbé J. A. (1906). *Hindu Manners, Customs and Ceremonies,* tr. Henry K. Beauchamp. Oxford: Clarendon Press.
Dumont, Louis (1972). *Homo Hierarchicus.* London: Paladin.
Dumont, Louis (1983). 'The debt to ancestors and the category of *sapiṇḍa*'. In Malamoud (1983: 1-20).
Dushkin, Lelah (1972). 'Scheduled caste politics'. *The Untouchables in Contemporary India,* ed. J. M. Mahar. Tucson: University of Arizona Press. 165-226.
Eck, Diana (1983). *Banaras: City of Light.* London: Routledge & Kegan Paul.
Edgerton, F. (1944). *The Bhagavad Gītā.* Cambridge, Mass.: Harvard University Press.
Entwistle, A. W. (1987). *Braj: Centre of Krishna Pilgrimage.* Groningen: Egbert Forsten.
Evison, Gillian (1989). 'Indian death rituals: the enactment of ambivalence'. Unpublished PhD thesis, University of Oxford.
Farquhar, J.N. (1920). *An Outline of the Religious Literature of India.* Oxford: Clarendon Press.
Firth, Shirley (1989). 'The good death: approaches to death, dying and bereavement among British Hindus'. *Perpectives on Death and Dying,* ed. Arthur Berger. Philadephia: Charles Press. 66-83.
Forbes, Geraldine H. (1975). *Positivism in Bengal.* Calcutta: Minerva.
Ghose, Manomohan (tr.) (1977). *Essentials of Dharma by Bankim Chandra Chatterjee.* Calcutta: Sribhumi Publishing Co.
Gold, Ann G. (1989). *Fruitful Journeys: The Ways of Rajasthani Pilgrims.* Delhi: Oxford University Press.
Gonda, J. (1967). *The Meaning of the Sanskrit Term* Dhāman. Amsterdam: North Holland.
Gopal, Rao (1959). *India of the Vedic Kalpasūtras.* Varanasi: Motilal Banarsidas.
Hacker, Paul (1958). 'Der Dharma-begriff des Neuhinduismus'. *Zeitschrift für Missions- und Religionswissenschaft 42.* 1-15.
Haldar, M. K. (1974). *Bankim on Equality.* Nedlands: Centre for Asian Studies, University of Western Australia.

Irving, B. A. (1853). *The Theory and Practice of Caste*. London: Smith, Elder & Co.
Isaacs, Harold R. (1965). *India's Ex-Untouchables*. New York: John Day.
Iyer, Raghavan (ed.) (1986). *The Moral and Political Writings of Mahatma Gandhi, Vol. II: Truth and Non-Violence*. Oxford: Clarendon Press.
Jackson, Robert, and Killingley, Dermot (1988). *Approaches to Hinduism*. London: John Murray.
Jordens, J. T. F. (1978). *Dayānanda Sarasvatī: His Life and Ideas*. Delhi: Oxford University Press.
Kane, Pandurang Vaman (1941). *A History of Dharmaśāstra, Vol. II*. Poona: Bhandarkar Oriental Research Institute. 2 parts, paginated continuously.
Kane, Pandurang Vaman (1953). *A History of Dharmaśāstra, Vol. IV*. Poona: Bhandarkar Oriental Research Institute.
Kane, Pandurang Vaman (1962). *A History of Dharmaśāstra, Vol. V*. Poona: Bhandarkar Oriental Research Institute. 2 parts, paginated continuously.
Kanitkar, H. and Jackson, R. (1982). *Hindus in Britain*. London: School of Oriental and African Studies.
Kaushik, Meena (1976). 'The symbolic representation of death'. *Contributions to Indian Sociology (NS) 10*. 265-92.
Killingley, D. H. (1977). 'Rammohun Roy's interpretation of the Vedānta'. Unpublished PhD thesis, University of London.
Killingley, D. M. (1990). *Farewell the Plumed Troop: A Memoir of the Indian Cavalry 1919-1945*. Newcastle upon Tyne: Grevatt & Grevatt.
King, Ursula (1977). 'True and perfect religion: Bankim Chandra Chatterjee's reinterpretation of Hinduism'. *Religion 7*. 127-48.
Klass, Morton (1980). *Caste: The Emergence of the South Asian Social System*. Philadephia: Institute for the Study of Human Issues.
Knipe, D. M. (1977). 'Sapiṇḍīkaraṇa: the Hindu rite of entry into heaven'. *Religious Encounters with Death: Insights from the History and Anthropology of Religion*, ed. E. Reynolds and F. Waugh. University Park: Pennsylvania State University Press. 112-24.
Knott, Kim (1986). *Hinduism in Leeds: A Study of Religious Practice in the Indian Hindu Community and in Hindu Related Groups*. Leeds: Department of Theology and Religious Studies, University of Leeds.
Leslie, Julia (1991). 'Suttee or sati: victim or victor?' *Roles and Rituals for Hindu Women*, ed. J. Leslie. London: Pinter. 175-91.
Lyons, John (1968). *Introduction to Theoretical Linguistics*. Cambridge: Cambridge University Press.
Macdonell, A. A., and Keith, A. B. (1912). *A Vedic Index of Names and Subjects*. 2 vols. Oxford: Clarendon Press. Reprinted Delhi: Motilal Banarsidass, 1958.
McDonald, Merryle. 'Rituals of motherhood among Gujarati women in East London'. In Burghart (ed.) (1987: 50-66).
Madan, T. N. (1987). *Non-renunciation: Themes and Interpretations of Hindu Culture*. Delhi: Oxford University Press.
Malamoud, Charles (1983). 'The theology of debt in Brahmanism'. In Malamoud (ed.) (1983: 21-40).
Malamoud, Charles (ed.) (1983). *Debts and Debtors*. Delhi: Vikas.
Mandelbaum, D. G. (1970). *Society in India*. 2 vols., paginated continuously. Berkeley: University of California Press.
Mangalamurugesan, N. K. (1980). *Self-Respect Movement in Tamil Nadu 1920-1940*. Madurai: Koodal.
Mayer, A.C. (1960). *Caste and Kinship in Central India*. London: Routledge & Kegan Paul.
Menski, W. F. (1983). 'Is there a customary form of widow-remarriage for Hindus?' *Kerala Law Times*, Journal Section. 69-72.
Menski, W. F. (1984). 'Role and ritual in the Hindu marriage'. Unpublished PhD thesis, University of London.
Menski, W. F. (1987). 'Legal pluralism in the Hindu marriage'. In Burghart (1987: 180-200).

Menski, W. F. (1988a). 'English family law and ethnic laws in Britain'. *Kerala Law Times,* 1988 (1), Journal Section. 56-66.
Menski, W. F. (1988b). 'Uniformity of laws in India and England'. *Journal of Law and Society 7 (11).* 11-26.
Menski, W. F. (1991). 'Asians in Britain and the question of adaptation to a new legal order: Asian laws in Britain?'. *Ethnicity, Identity, Migration: The South Asian Context,* ed. M. Israel. Toronto: Center for South Asian Studies.
Mitra, Abhijit (1979). 'Bhudev Mukhopadhyay: the beginning of Indian sociology'. *The Bengali Intellectual Tradition,* ed. A. K. Mukhopadhyaya. Calcutta: K. P. Bagchi. 81-109.
Monier-Williams, M. (1884). *Brahmanism and Hinduism.* London: John Murray.
Monier-Williams, M. (1899). *A Sanskrit-English Dictionary,* 2nd edn. Oxford: Clarendon Press.
Mukhopadhyaya, Sujit Kumar (1960). *The Vajrasūcī of Aśvaghoṣa,* 2nd edn. Santiniketan: Vishwabharati University.
National Council of Hindu Temples (U.K.) (1987). *Hindu Funeral Rites.* Leicester: Shree Sanatan Mandir, Weymouth St.
OED. A New English Dictionary. Oxford: Clarendon Press, 1884-1928, re-issued as *The Oxford English Dictionary,* 1933.
Padfield, J. (1896). *The Hindu at Home: Being Sketches of Hindu Daily Life.* London: Simkin, Marshall, Hamilton, Kent & Co.
Pandey, R. B. (1969). *Hindu Saṃskāras: Socio-religious Study of the Hindu Sacraments,* 2nd edn. Delhi: Motilal Banarsidass.
Parry, Jonathan (1979). *Caste and Kinship in Kangra.* London: Routledge & Kegan Paul.
Parry, Jonathan (1982). 'Sacrificial death and the necrophagous ascetic'. *Death and the Regeneration of Life,* ed. M. Block and J. Parry. Cambridge University Press. 74-110.
Parry, Jonathan (1985). 'Death and the digestion: the symbolism of food and eating in North Indian mortuary rites'. *Man (NS) 20.* 612-30.
Pearl, David (1986). *Family Law and the Immigrant Communities.* Bristol. Jordan and Sons.
Phillimore, P. (1991). 'Unmarried women of the Dhaula Dhar: celibacy and social control in north-west India'. *Journal of Anthropological Research 47 (3).*
Pitt-Rivers, Julian (1971). 'On the word "caste"'. *The Translation of Culture. Essays to E. E. Evans-Pritchard,* ed. T. O. Beidelman. London: Tavistock, 231-56.
Planalp, J. (1956). 'Religious life and values in a North Indian village', Part 2. Unpublished PhD thesis, Cornell University.
Poulter, Sebastian (1986). *English Law and Ethnic Minority Customs.* London: Butterworth.
Price, Pamela (1979). 'Resources and rule in zamindari South India, 1802-1903: Sivaganga and Ramnad as kingdoms under the raj'. Unpublished PhD thesis, University of Madison, Wisconsin.
Quayle, Brendan, Phillimore, Peter and Good, Anthony (1980). *Hindu Death and the Ritual Journey* (Durham Working Papers in Social Anthropology 4). Durham: Department of Anthropology, University of Durham.
Radhakrishnan, S. (1940). *Eastern Religions and Western Thought,* 2nd edn. London: Oxford University Press (1st edn 1939).
Radhakrishnan, S. (1960). *The Hindu View of Life.* London: Allen & Unwin (1st edn. 1927).
Radhakrishnan, S. (1947). Religion and Society. London, Allen & Unwin.
Ramamohana: *Rāmamohana Granthābalī,* ed. Brajendranath Banerji and Sajanīkānta Dās. 7 parts separately paginated, bound in one. Calcutta: Baṅgīya Sāhitya Pariṣat, 1952.
Rammohun: *The English Works of Raja Rammohun Roy,* ed. Kalidas Nag and Debjyoti Burman. 6 vols. Calcutta: Sadharan Brahmo Samaj, 1945-51. Short titles or descriptions of individual works are included in the references to this collection.

Raychaudhuri, Tapan (1988). *Europe Reconsidered: Perceptions of the West in Nineteenth Century Bengal.* Delhi: Oxford University Press.
Renou, Louis (1960). *Le destin du Véda dans l'Inde.* Paris: E. de Boccard.
Risley, H. H. (1891). *The tribes and castes of Bengal.* 2 vols. Calcutta: Bengal Secretariat Press.
Sarma, Jyotirmoyee (1980). *Caste Dynamics among the Bengali Hindus.* Calcutta: Firma K. L. Mukhopadhyay.
Śāstrī, Sivanath (1975). 'Caste division' (Jātibhed), lecture in Calcutta, 1884; English tr in *The Indian Magazine Nos. 237-9,* London, 1889. Reprinted in *Nineteenth-century Studies 10.* 245-75.
Schwartzberg, J. E. (ed.) (1978). *A Historical Atlas of South Asia.* Chicago: University of Chicago Press.
Sen, P. K. (1950). *Biography of a New Faith, vol. I.* Calcutta: Thacker, Spink & Co. (Vol. II 1954).
Sharma, Ursula (1971). *Rampal and His Family.* London: Collins.
Shastri, Dakshina Ranjan (1963). *Origin and Development of the Rituals of Ancestor Worship in India.* Calcutta: Bookland.
Sinha, Pradip (1965). *Nineteenth Century Bengal: Aspects of Social History.* Calcutta: Firma K. L. Mukhopadhyay.
Smith, Vincent (1958). *The Oxford History of India,* 3rd edn. Oxford: Clarendon Press. (1st edn 1919.)
Srinivas, M. N. (1962). *Caste in Modern India and Other Essays.* London: Asia Publishing House.
Srinivas, M. N. (1965). *Religion and Society among the Coorgs of South India.* Bombay: Asia Publishing House.
Stevenson, Mrs. S. (1920). *The Rites of the Twice-born.* London: Oxford University Press.
Tambiah, S. J. (1973). 'From varṇa to caste through mixed unions'. *The Character of Kinship,* ed. Jack Goody. Cambridge: Cambridge University Press. 191-229.
Tilak, B. G. (1922). *Bal Gangadhar Tilak: His Writings and Speeches.* Madras: Ganesh.
Van Gennep, A. (1960). *The Rites of Passage,* tr. M. B. Vizedom and G. L. Caffee. Chicago: University of Chicago Press. (*Les rites de passage,* 1908.)
Vivekānanda: *The Complete Works of Swami Vivekananda.* Calcutta: Advaita Ashrama, 1977. 8 vols. Some earlier editions have different contents and pagination. Short titles or descriptions of individual works are included in the references to this collection.
Wadia, A. R. (1952). 'The social philosophy of Radhakrishnan'. *The Philosophy of Sarvepalli Radhakrishnan,* ed. P. A. Schilpp. New York: Tudor. 755-85.
Weber, Max (1958). *The Religion of India: The Sociology of Hinduism and Buddhism.* New York: Free Press.
Winternitz, M. (1927). *A History of Sanskrit Literature, vol I,* tr. S. Ketkar. Calcutta: University of Calcutta.
Yule, Henry and Burnell, A. C. (1903). *Hobson-Jobson: A Glossary of Anglo-Indian Words and Phrases,* 2nd edn. London: Routledge & Kegan Paul.

INDEX